T0332940

Managing Security Services in Heterogenous Networks

Managing Security Services in Heterogenous Networks

Confidentiality, Integrity, Availability, Authentication, and Access Control

Edited by Dr. N. Jeyanthi,
Dr. Kun Ma, Dr. Thinagaran Perumal,
and Dr. R. Thandeeswaran

CRC Press
Taylor & Francis Group
Boca Raton London New York

CRC Press is an imprint of the
Taylor & Francis Group, an **informa** business

First edition published 2021
by CRC Press
6000 Broken Sound Parkway NW, Suite 300, Boca Raton, FL 33487-2742

and by CRC Press
2 Park Square, Milton Park, Abingdon, Oxon, OX14 4RN

© 2021 Taylor & Francis Group, LLC

CRC Press is an imprint of Taylor & Francis Group, LLC

ISBN: 9780367457341 (hbk)
ISBN: 9781003034049 (ebk)

Typeset in Caslon
by MPS Limited, Dehradun

Contents

1

ACCESS CONTROL METHODS IN CLOUD ENABLED THE CLOUD-ENABLED INTERNET OF THINGS

B. RAVINDER REDDY, T. ADILAKSHMI, AND C. PAVAN KUMAR

*Department of Computer Science and
Engineering, Anurag Group of
Institutions, Hyderabad, Telangana
Department of Computer Science and
Engineering, Vasavi College of
Engineering, Hyderabad, Telangana
Department of Computer Science and
Engineering, Indian Institute of
Information Technology Dharwad,
Karnataka*

Contents

The Internet of Things (IoT) happens to be one of the most promising technologies in recent research. Collecting data from multiple heterogeneous devices, as well as storage and analysis of the collected data, has applications in many domains such as healthcare, transportation, home automation, etc., drawing the attention of researchers from various domains. Even though data are collected from different heterogeneous devices, these data are stored in the cloud. In case of the cloud-enabled Internet of Things, it offers multitenancy as one of its characteristics. Simultaneously securing such data and offering a good access control policy over the cloud without compromising on user data and privacy is a challenging task. Access control policies provide an efficient access control mechanism for users to access data over the cloud. In this chapter, an extensive overview of existing access control policies proposed in the context of the cloud and IoT are discussed in detail. Also, the possibilities of future research directions are outlined.

1.1 Introduction

The IoT is state-of-the-art technology that not only requires the development of infrastructure and software but also the design and deployment of services capable of supporting multiple scalable, interoperable, and secure applications. In the process of designing the secure communication architecture for IoT data, many have realized that a common problem to be addressed is the security of the information, with an emphasis on access control policies so that data can be used effectively by a wide range of users based on their requirements.

In this chapter, we review and summarize recent trends and challenges in access control related to data in the cloud and IoT and discuss various models that support data accessibility, taking the IoT and cloud computing as reference examples of application domains.

The Internet Society [31] describes the IoT as follows: "IoT refers to scenarios in which network connectivity and computing capability to extend it to objects, sensors and devices not normally considered computing devices, allowing these to generate exchange and utilize data with no human intervention".

Mattern and Floerkemeier [23] visualized IoT technology as "The Internet of Things represents a vision in which the Internet extends into the real world embracing everyday objects. Physical items are no longer disconnected from the virtual world, but can be controlled remotely and can act as physical access points to Internet services".

1.1.1 The Network of Things

The National Institute of Standards and Technology (NIST) defines the following five primitives for the "Network of Things" that includes IoT as well [35]:

1. *Sensors* that measure the physical parameters that are of interest such as temperature, humidity, pressure, weight, etc.
2. *Aggregators* that convert the raw data into processed or aggregated data.
3. *Communication channel* that allows data transmission among the entities involved.
4. *External utilities* include external components required for the computation.
5. *Decision triggera* are predicates that have true values used to initiate a command or action.

The IoT may or may not utilize all the primitives defined for the Network of Things, dor example, a cyber physical system that can operate without the help of sensors. Another essential primitive component required for the IoT (not listed in the NIST primitives) is "*smartness*". Research in IoT is evolving in multiple directions with the research progress in the IoT primitives and manufacture of energy-efficient, low-cost hardware communication devices [20]. However, the heterogeneity of underlying devices and communication technologies, interoperability, and security requirements in different layers is a challenge for generic IoT solutions to be developed on a larger scale.

Xu et al. [11] proposed a four-layered architecture for IoT comprising the following:

1. Sensing Layer – Acts as an interface between the physical world and cyber world, sensing and collecting data with the help of sensors, cameras, radio frequency identification (RFID), etc.
2. Networking Layer – Provides networking support for data transmission and collection and control applications.
3. Service Layer – Acts as middleware to support business logic and service integration.
4. Interface Layer – Provides an interface to seamlessly integrate the service layer with end users.

1.2 The IoT Application Domain

The IoT has applications in various domains. Figure 1.1 represents an overview of IoT application areas ranging from personal gadgets to industries.

1.3 Cloud Computing

The IoT infrastructure collects data and stores them over networked servers like the cloud. According to NIST, cloud computing [24] is defined as "a model for enabling ubiquitous, convenient, on-demand network access to a shared pool of configurable computing resources that can be rapidly provisioned and released with minimal management effort or service provider interaction".

Also, NIST suggests essential characteristics, deployment models, and service models for cloud computing [24].

1.3.1 Essential Characteristics

a. On-demand self service
b. Broad network access
c. Resource pooling

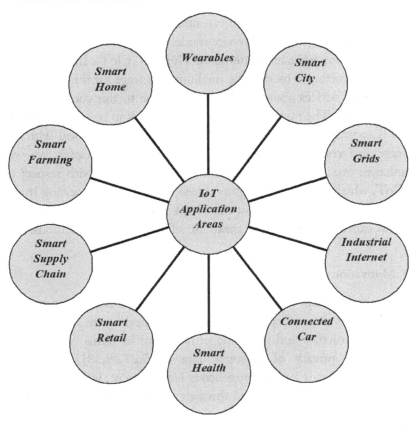

Figure 1.1 Application of IoT in various domains.

d.   Rapid elasticity
e.   Measured service

1.3.2 Deployment Models

a. Public cloud
b. Private cloud
c. Hybrid cloud
d. Community cloud

1.3.3 Service Models

a. Software as a Service (SaaS)
b. Platform as a Service (PaaS)
c. Infrastructure as a Service (IaaS)

The connected things ecosystem can utilize any of the previously mentioned cloud deployment and service models in combination to store data to form the Cloud-Enabled Internet of Things (CEIoT). In CEIoT, the cloud infrastructure is used as the medium of storage for the data sensed through IoT devices; many challenges arise due to this combination of IoT and cloud. The most common issue that needs to be ensured at both ends is security and privacy, as both the cloud and IoT deal with the storage and collection of data, respectively. In this chapter, we will emphasize one of the security features, access control, with respect to CEIoT, which validates the righteousness of the user in accessing stored data on the cloud. Throughout this chapter we have provided an overview of existing methods that make use of access control methods.

1.4 Motivation

The main motivation behind this chapter is the basic concept that heterogeneous data collected through sensing devices are stored on the cloud infrastructure and need the utmost care in terms of providing security and privacy of personal data [9,15,27,29,38]. The cloud being a multitenant and heterogeneous environment, it will be storing different types of data collected through various sources. Ensuring security to such data is of the utmost priority, as a simple breach can lead to discrepancies in business entities that trust the infrastructure as a medium of storage. CIA (confidentiality, integrity, and availability) traits are the essential components to ensure the security of data. These features are also important for providing proper access control, which determines information security [21,30,32,37].

1.5 Preliminaries

The primitives used in defining secure access control policies are discussed in this section.

1.5.1 Role-Based Access Control

Role-based access control (RBAC) methods have been predominantly used since the UNIX operating system days to specify permission to a specific set of users to access files [12]. With the recent awareness and advances in the technology, many of the commercial applications or vendors have come up with their own access control policies suitable for their products or organizations. RBAC has evolved from mandatory access control (MAC) and discretionary access control (DAC).

DAC refers to restricting or permitting access based on the group to which the initiator of the action belongs. For example, a user belonging to group A may or may not be given permission to access some set of files based on his or her membership in group A.

MAC implementation requires specifying user permissions at the time of user creation itself. For example, a set of users in an organization is allowed to access the kernel of the operating system, whereas another set of users is strictly denied such access. MAC methods are widely used in defining multilevel security and military applications.

RBAC methods define roles to users and vice versa. Many vendors and practitioners have proposed their own RBAC policies [33]. In order to standardize the RBAC model, Ferraiolo et al. [13] have proposed NIST standards for RBAC, with the RBAC reference model defining a collection of components. The RBAC model considers users, roles, permissions, operations, and objects as its elements.

The following components are defined for the RBAC reference model [13]:

1. Core RBAC – A minimalistic definition of RBAC with its elements consisting of users, roles, permissions, operations and objects, and their functionalities. It operates in a user-role review model wherein users are assigned to a specific role and roles are assigned to a specific user.
2. Hierarchical RBAC – Defines role hierarchies and structuring roles in an organization. It can also define inheritance among roles.

   A further two types are defined in hierarchical RBAC:

   a. General Hierarchical RBAC – It supports hierarchical and multiple inherited permissions to a user.
   b. Limited Hierarchical RBAC – It supports limiting access to

users. An access structure such as trees or inverted trees can be used to define access permissions.

3. Static Separation of Duty Relations

   a. Static Separation of Duty (SSD) – This will place constraints on the assignment of users to roles. It can be used to prevent assigning contradictory (or mutually exclusive) roles to a single user.
   b. Static Separation of Duty in the Presence of a Hierarchy – This is similar to SSD and can be used to assign permissions hierarchically in addition to direct asssignment of permissions.

4. Dynamic Separation of Duty Relations – This can be used to limit the number of permissions and roles to a user and timely revocation of permissions.

Out of which implementation of core RBAC component ensures full-fledged RBAC implementations, based on requirements other components can be introduced on top of the core RBAC. For detailed efforts on the standardization of RBAC, refer to [13].

1.5.2 Capability-Based Access Control

In the capability-based access control (CapBAC) method, a user in need of a service will place a request (containing the user's attribute, resource ID, etc.) to grant access permission [16,18]. The policy decision point (PDP) evaluates the request and compares it with the knowledge base it possess. If the request is accepted, then PDP will issue a capability token (in the form of a ticket or token) to grant permission to the requested resource. Upon receiving the capability, the user can directly request the resource provider to access the resource. It is similar to the Kereberos mechanism [25].

CapBAC also guarantees the principle of least authority (PoLA) wherein a user will be enabled with the least access permissions he or she requires to complete a task and nothing more. In addition, the CapBAC method can outsource the authorization process, which was not present in the RBAC model. Also, the access policy logic can be locally defined based on requirements in this model, or a context-aware access control policy can be defined.

One of the drawbacks in both RBAC and CapBAC is a single point of failure. If a server or service authenticating user requests is down, the system will not be in a position to serve requests. Recently some distributed architectures have been proposed to overcome this drawback. RBAC is more generic in nature and can be adopted to any enterprise or communication setup that requires RBAC, whereas CapBAC mechanisms can be defined specific to applications.

1.5.3 Attribute-Based Access Control

Attribute-based access control (ABAC) is also called policy-based access control [19]. In ABAC, both subjects and objects will have attributes of their own in addition to action and environment. A subject possessing a set of attributes will request a central entity to give permission to access a particular object. The central entity will have policy definitions on "who can access what". The central entity will evaluate subject requests with respect to object attributes and grant or reject access considering the action and environment.

ABAC will have a central entity describing policies. Every time it is not required to define new policies for the individual subjects, only attributes belonging to a subject can be changed. This will enable the central entity to efficiently handle group dynamics, a core feature that is required for IoT applications.

Even though the standards for ABAC are in a draft stage by NIST and other standards associations, the majority of ABAC models have the following components, as outlined by Servos and Osborn [34]:

a. Subject
b. Object
c. Attributes
d. Permissions
e. Policies

The core ABAC can be extended in many directions and environments. One of the well-researched and distinct areas of research that has evolved out of ABAC is attribute-based encryption (ABE) with ciphertext policy ABE (CPABE) [5] and key policy ABE (KPABE) [14,36] types. As ABE techniques are beyond the scope of this chapter, a detailed description on the same can be found in.

1.6 Access Control Methods in the CEIoT

The CEIoT is one of the upcoming research areas that recently caught the attention of researchers in various domains such as IoT, cloud computing, and access control methods [2,10,26]. Many architectures have been proposed in the literature and practice for IoT even though there is no consensus among the architectures [28,30]. In general, the proposed architectures consist of an object layer and application layer in addition to one or more middle layers. The object layer corresponds to physical devices (such as sensors, cameras, RFID tags, smart phones, etc.) from which data are collected. The application layer consists of services offered over data collected such as data access, analytics, decision support system, data trade, etc. [1,22]. The middle layer is composed of single or multiple layers that in turn comprise the network layer or similar supporting layers of communication for the IoT framework. Some architectures even have additional sublayers to the middle layers.

Gubbi et al. [15] proposed the integration of cloud computing as one of the layers existing between the object layer and application layer in addition to other layers. However, these methods do not address access control methods. In this section, we review the schemes that satisfy CEIoT criteria. Even though the schemes proposed do not employ a cloud computing layer, they are reviewed as they offer CapBAC in the IoT, which can be extended to incorporate a cloud computing layer.

1.6.1 The Cloud-Enabled Internet of Things

Alshehri and Sandhu [2] proposed cloud-enabled access control methods for the IoT. As discussed in the previous section, in many of the IoT architectures only the object layer and

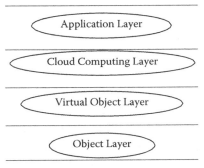

Figure 1.2 Access control–oriented IoT architecture proposed by Alshehri and Sandhu.

application layer were proposed initially, and later Gubbi et al. proposed a cloud computing layer to the IoT architecture to exploit the features of cloud computing. To enable access control in CEIoT, Alshehri and Sandhu proposed a four-layer architecture, as given in Figure. 1.2 and named it access control–oriented IoT (ACOIoT) architecture [2].

Alshehri and Sandhu explained this architecture with the help of a multivalue switch case and other such multiple devices [2]. Access control logic will be present in the cloud computing layer, and they have adopted ABAC for access control. The cloud computing layer offers multitenancy and a different type of structured and unstructured data management support [17]. The object layer will consist of heterogeneous devices that collect data such as sensors, camera, smart phones (with multiple sensors), and actuators and present data to the upper layers, namely the virtual layer. The virtual layer consists of virtual objects that are mapped to object-layer devices. Virtual-layer objects can be defined as required. Virtual objects help to store the state or values associated with devices in the object layer. The virtual object layer is also used to communicate commands to the object layer from higher layers. Virtual objects can be defined either as one to one (one virtual object mapped to one device) or one to many (one virtual object mapped to many devices). ABAC in the ACOIoT architecture use case is demonstrated with a multivalue switch case. The PDP and policies will be stored in the cloud computing layer.

Further, Alshehri and Sandhu [3] extended the architecture in [2] to access control in cars and propose operational models for virtual object (VO) communication.

1.6.1.1 CEIoT for Wearable Devices   Bhatt et al. [7] extended the architecture in [2] to wearable devices with an additional object abstraction layer (in between the object layer and virtual object layer) to efficiently implement access control policies with specifications on interlayer communication (specifying which layers are allowed and not allowed to communicate with each other). Wearable devices are personal devices, and providing access control in such a resource-constrained device environment is challenging.

1.6.1.2 Authorization in the Cloud-Based IoT   Bhatt et al. [6] also extended the architecture proposed in [2] to handle present-day authorization processes in an IoT scenario. Bhatt et al. [6] demonstrated an enhanced ACOIoT (EACOIoT) in implementing access policies. An additional object abstraction layer present in this model will handle authorization and privacy between the object layer and upper layers of the EACOIoT framework. An object abstraction layer consisting of gateway devices provides abstraction between devices in the object layer and virtual object layer. The EACOIoT framework is demonstrated with the help of smart home and smart university parking use cases.

1.6.1.3 Amazon Web Services–Enabled IoT   Bhatt et al. [8] extended this model to IoT devices connected to the Amazon Web Services (AWS) cloud and proposed ABAC for defining access control logic. They have considered a thermostat and light bulbs use case to demonstrate AWS IoT access control. This model is proposed even considering communication protocols such as MQTT. A virtual object associated with devices in the object layer is termed a "shadow" or "things shadow".

1.6.2 Capability-Based Access Control in the IoT

Even though there is no direct work involving the cloud computing layer in CapBAC, the models proposed by Gusmeroli et al. [16] and Hernandez-Ramos et al. [18] in the IoT context are discussed in this sectiona as these models can be directly extended to models involving the cloud computing layer.

1.6.2.1 Centralized Capability-Based IoT Gusmeroli et al. [16] proposed a centralized capability-based access control in the IoT (CapBACIoT). To address the scalability and group dynamic drawbacks in RBAC and ABAC, Gusmeroli et al. [16] proposed the CapBAC model in the IoT. They have adopted this approach because CapBAC provides better delegation support, capability revocation (temporal revocation), and information granularity with a single PDP. They demonstrate this model with information and service access associated with car and housekeeping use cases. However, this approach has not outlined how access logic is defined separately for different devices, which is very much required in the case of IoT, as the access policy of one device may or may not be same as that of another device.

1.6.2.2 Distributed Capability-Based IoT Hernandez-Ramos et al. [18] proposed a distributed approach for implementation of CapBAC in IoT. Distributed CapABC in the IoT architecture overcomes the drawbacks of a single PDP in the centralized CapBAC approach and proposed access logic independently from each of the end devices based on requirements. Hernandez-Ramos et al. [18] have even implemented the proposed scheme on a 32-bit RISC processor and demonstrated its sustainability in the IoT. Also, they have discussed end-to-end secure communication adopting elliptic curve cryptography (ECC).

1.7 Future Scope

The access control models defined here are restricted to one type of environment. On a large scale, there are lots of implementation setbacks that arise, many research challenges, and opportunity for future. As considered in this chapter, the state-of-the-art infrastructures like cloud and IoT need a higher level of security, being also robust at the ground level. Even the existing advanced access control policies lack in some properties that are essential, like improper multitenant architecture, standardization of the overall policy architecture, effective collection of heterogeneous data, boosting the power and energy efficiency for the IoT infrastructure, Big Data collection, storage and maintenance, security and privacy of data, pricing and billing cloud storage, scalability and flexibility of the resources utilized, necessity for distributed and decentralized architectures, trustless authentication such as the application of smart contract for access control, avoidance of a central authority, anonymity of users, applying homomorphic encryption, and much more.

1.8 Conclusion

An overview of access control methods in the CEIoT, along with different access control models, were discussed in this chapter. Existing models, relevant reference sources, and possible research directions were also discussed. This chapter serves as a pointer to researchers interested in working in the area of access control in the CEIoT.

References

1. Ejaz Ahmed, Ibrar Yaqoob, Ibrahim Abaker Targio Hashem, Imran Khan, Abdelmuttlib Ibrahim Abdalla Ahmed, Muhammad Imran, and Athanasios V Vasilakos. The role of big data analytics in internet of things. *Computer Networks*, 129:459–471, 2017.
2. Asma Alshehri and Ravi Sandhu. Access control models for cloud-enabled internet of things: A proposed architecture and research agenda. In *2016 IEEE 2nd International Conference on Collaboration and Internet Computing (CIC)*, pages 530–538. IEEE, 2016.
3. Asma Alshehri and Ravi Sandhu. Access control models for virtual object communication in cloud-enabled iot. In *2017 IEEE International Conference on Information Reuse and Integration (IRI)*, pages 16–25. IEEE, 2017.
4. Luigi Atzori, Antonio Iera, and Giacomo Morabito. The internet of things: A survey. *Computer Networks*, 54(15):2787–2805, 2010.
5. John Bethencourt, Amit Sahai, and Brent Waters. Ciphertext- policy attribute-based encryption. In *2007 IEEE Symposium on Security and Privacy (SP'07)*, pages 321–334. IEEE, 2007.
6. Smriti Bhatt, A Tawalbeh Loai, Pankaj Chhetri, and Paras Bhatt. Authorizations in cloud-based internet of things: current trends and use cases. In *2019 Fourth International Conference on Fog and Mobile Edge Computing (FMEC)*, pages 241–246. IEEE, 2019.
7. Smriti Bhatt, Farhan Patwa, and Ravi Sandhu. An access control framework for cloud-enabled wearable internet of things. In *2017 IEEE 3rd International Conference on Collaboration and Internet Computing (CIC)*, pages 328–338. IEEE, 2017.
8. Smriti Bhatt, Farhan Patwa, and Ravi Sandhu. Access control model for aws internet of things. In *International Conference on Network and System Security*, pages 721–736. Springer, 2017.
9. Alessio Botta, Walter De Donato, Valerio Persico, and Antonio Pescape. Integration of cloud computing and internet of things: a survey. *Future Generation Computer Systems*, 56:684–700, 2016.
10. Luis Cruz-Piris, Diego Rivera, Ivan Marsa-Maestre, Enrique De La Hoz, and Juan R Velasco. Access control mechanism for iot environments based on modelling communication procedures as resources. *Sensors*, 18(3):917, 2018.
11. Li Da Xu, Wu He, and Shancang Li. Internet of things in industries: A survey. *IEEE Transactions on Industrial Informatics*, 10(4): 2233–2243, 2014.
12. Glenn Faden. Rbac in unix administration. In *Proceedings of the Fourth ACM Workshop on Role-based Access Control*, pages 95–101, 1999.
13. David F Ferraiolo, Ravi Sandhu, Serban Gavrila, D Richard Kuhn, and Ramaswamy Chandramouli. Proposed nist standard for role- based access control. *ACM Transactions on Information and System Security (TISSEC)*, 4(3):224–274, 2001.

14. Vipul Goyal, Omkant Pandey, Amit Sahai, and Brent Waters. Attribute-based encryption for fine-grained access control of encrypted data. In *Proceedings of the 13th ACM Conference on Computer and Communications Security*, pages 89–98, 2006.

15. Jayavardhana Gubbi, Rajkumar Buyya, Slaven Marusic, and Marimuthu Palaniswami. Internet of things (iot): A vision, architectural elements, and future directions. *Future Generation Computer Systems*, 29(7): 1645–1660, 2013.

16. Sergio Gusmeroli, Salvatore Piccione, and Domenico Rotondi. A capability-based security approach to manage access control in the internet of things. *Mathematical and Computer Modelling*, 58(5-6): 1189–1205, 2013.

17. Ibrahim Abaker Targio Hashem, Ibrar Yaqoob, Nor Badrul Anuar, Salimah Mokhtar, Abdullah Gani, and Samee Ullah Khan. The rise of big data on cloud computing: Review and open research issues. *Information Systems*, 47:98–115, 2015.

18. Jose L Hernandez-Ramos, Antonio J Jara, and Antonio F Skarmeta. Distributed capability-based access control for the internet of things. *Journal of Internet Services and Information Security (JISIS)*, 3(3/4):1–16.

19. Vincent C Hu, David Ferraiolo, Rick Kuhn, Arthur R Friedman, Alan J Lang, Margaret M Cogdell, Adam Schnitzer, Kenneth Sandlin, Robert Miller, Karen Scarfone, et al. Guide to attribute based access control (abac) definition and considerations (draft). *NIST special publication*, 800(162), 2013.

20. Amy Loutfi, Arne Jonsson, Lars Karlsson, Leili Lind, Maria Linden, Federico Pecora, and Thiemo Voigt. Ecare@ home: a distributed research environment on semantic interoperability. In *International Conference on IoT Technologies for HealthCare*, pages 3–8. Springer, 2016.

21. Carsten Maple. Security and privacy in the internet of things. *Journal of Cyber Policy*, 2(2):155–184, 2017.

22. Mohsen Marjani, Fariza Nasaruddin, Abdullah Gani, Ahmad Karim, Ibrahim Abaker Targio Hashem, Aisha Siddiqa, and Ibrar Yaqoob. Big iot data analytics: architecture, opportunities, and open research challenges. *IEEE Access*, 5:5247–5261, 2017.

23. Friedemann Mattern and Christian Floerkemeier. From the internet of computers to the internet of things. In *From active data management to event-based systems and more*, pages 242–259. Springer, 2010.

24. Peter Mell, Tim Grance, et al. The nist definition of cloud computing. *NIST Special Publication*, 800(415):1–7, 2011.

25. B Clifford Neuman and Theodore Ts'o. Kerberos: An authentication service for computer networks. *IEEE Communications Magazine*, 32(9):33–38, 1994.

26. Aafaf Ouaddah, Hajar Mousannif, Anas Abou Elkalam, and Abdellah Ait Ouahman. Access control in the internet of things: Big challenges and new opportunities. *Computer Networks*, 112:237– 262, 2017.

27. Pritee Parwekar. From internet of things towards cloud of things. In *2011 2nd International Conference on Computer and Communication Technology (ICCCT-2011)*, pages 329–333. IEEE, 2011.
28. Pawani Porambage, Mika Ylianttila, Corinna Schmitt, Pardeep Kumar, Andrei Gurtov, and Athanasios V Vasilakos. The quest for privacy in the internet of things. *IEEE Cloud Computing*, 3(2):36–45, 2016.
29. B B Prahlada Rao, Paval Saluia, Neetu Sharma, Ankit Mittal, and Shivay Veer Sharma. Cloud computing for internet of things & sensing based applications. In *2012 Sixth International Conference on Sensing Technology (ICST)*, pages 374–380. IEEE, 2012.
30. Partha Pratim Ray. A survey on internet of things architectures. *Journal of King Saud University-Computer and Information Sciences*, 30(3): 291–319, 2018.
31. Karen Rose, Scott Eldridge, and Lyman Chapin. The internet of things: An overview. *The Internet Society (ISOC)*, 80, 2015.
32. Pierangela Samarati and S De Capitani di Vimercati. Cloud security: Issues and concerns. *Encyclopedia on Cloud Computing*, pages 1–14, 2016.
33. Ravi S Sandhu, Edward J Coyne, Hal L Feinstein, and Charles E Youman. Role-based access control models. *Computer*, 29(2):38– 47, 1996.
34. Daniel Servos and Sylvia L Osborn. Current research and open problems in attribute-based access control. *ACM Computing Surveys (CSUR)*, 49(4):1–45, 2017.
35. Jeffrey Voas. Networks of things. *NIST Special Publication*, 800(183): 800–883, 2016.
36. Chang-Ji Wang and Jian-Fa Luo. A key-policy attribute-based encryption scheme with constant size ciphertext. In *2012 Eighth International Conference on Computational Intelligence and Security*, pages 447–451. IEEE, 2012.
37. Zhifeng Xiao and Yang Xiao. Security and privacy in cloud computing. *IEEE communications surveys & tutorials*, 15(2):843–859, 2012.
38. Wei Yu, Fan Liang, Xiaofei He, William Grant Hatcher, Chao Lu, Jie Lin, and Xinyu Yang. A survey on the edge computing for the internet of things. *IEEE access*, 6:6900–6919, 2017.

2

AN INTELLIGENT WEIGHTED FUZZY CLUSTER–BASED SECURE ROUTING ALGORITHM FOR MOBILE AD-HOC NETWORKS

K.P. RAMAPRABHA AND N. JEYANTHI

School of Information Technology and Engineering, VIT, Vellore, Tamil Nandu, India, njeyanthi@vit.ac.in

Contents

2.1 Introduction

The mobile ad-hoc network (MANET) is a wireless network which has a dynamic topology. Here, the nodes use peer-to-peer data transmission and multihop routes for communicating with each other in this network scenario. Moreover, there is no fixed infrastructure for data communication. The fixed infrastructure can be formed as a temporary static topology by forming a group (cluster) to communicate with all the neighbor nodes. This group-based communication is useful for providing better communication facility in many emerging scenarios such as battlefield communications, emergency operation, disaster relief, survival search, and sensor dust. But due to the dynamic topology and static topology changes of MANETs, designing secure and reliable routing protocols for those networks is a challenging process, especially in the large-scale network.

In clustering, the cluster head collects the data from its members, aggregates it, and transmits the aggregated data to the sink through a single-hop or multihop manner. Multihop routing provides an opportunity for the nodes to bring the malicious activity to MANETs. Security is also an important issue in MANETs due to the presence of a malicious node in the transmission path. These malicious nodes may drop the packets or misdirect the messages in routes or replay all the active routing packets from a valid node to forge the valid node's identity. Malicious nodes disrupt the network traffic by using the forged identity in routing. The trust evaluation process is an important task in the secure routing of MANETs. The trust scores are dynamically changed due to the occurrences of various attacks at different times in many paths. The trust score is the mathematical representation of the node's attitude in comparison to an another node in the network.

In this chapter, an intelligent weighted fuzzy cluster–based secure routing algorithm (IWFCSRA) is proposed ifor MANETs for enhancing the network lifetime and throughputs with security. Moreover, a fuzzy rule–based weighted distance–based outlier detection algorithm (FRWDOA) for distinguishing the outliers within the network is discussed. In this proposed work, new fuzzy rules have been generated with weights and used for forming clusters and also for calculating the trust scores, which are useful for making a final decision regarding the routing process. Moreover, the final trust paths for the respective clusters have been finalized based on the trust scores, energy, and weighted fuzzy rules in MANETs.

The remainder of this chapter is organized as follows: Section 2 provides the related works in the areas of secure routing protocols for MANETs. Section 3 describes in detail the proposed system architecture. Section 4 explains the details of the proposed model. Section 5 depicts the results obtained from this work and compares them with related work. Section 6 gives conclusions on this work and suggests some possible future works.

2.2 Related Works

In a wireless and ad-hoc network environment, secured and energy-fficient transmissions are needed to improve the network life-time and throughput. Clustering is a well-known technique for im-proving the energy efficiency in computer networks. Many works have been carried out in clustering techniques and are in the literature [1,6,10]. In multihop routing, secure transmission is very important. The malicious nodes in the route may attack the packets. So, many researchers have worked on secure routing and are in the literature [1,2,4]. Zhan et al. [5] proposed a trust-aware routing framework (TARF) to secure the WSNs from adversaries misdirecting the mul-tihop routing. TARF provides a trustworthy and energy-efficient route that protects WSNs from the harmful attacks exploiting the replay of routing information. In the past, Thippeswamy et al. [6] proposed a secure trust–aware energy-efficient adaptive routing (STEAR) pro-tocol for dynamic WSNs. STEAR effectively identifies the malicious nodes using a dynamic secret key, packet flow status, energy, and trust. However, considering the dynamic nature of attackers, it is necessary to work further to detect and prevent novel attacks.

Duan et al. [7] proposed a trust-aware secure routing framework (TSRF) to resist various attacks. The authors proposed a specific trust computation and trust derivation schemes to deal with the attacks. Their protocol considers the trust metric as well as QoS requirements in the path selection. Gu et al. [8] designed a secure communication protocol for end-to-end communication in WSNs. In their protocol, the differentiated key predistribution methodology was used to distribute the different number of keys to different sensors to enhance the resilience of certain links. Tang et al. [9] proposed a secure and efficient cost-aware secure routing (CASER) protocol to address the network optimization and security issues. However, a unique routing algorithm which considers energy and security based on trust is necessary to enhance the routing performance.

Souza and Varaprasad [10] proposed a multipath routing protocol for WSN using a digital signature crypto system for transmitting the data packets in a secure manner. Ganesh and Amutha [11] proposed an efficient and secure routing protocol through SNR-based dynamic clustering mechanisms (ESRPSDC). In their work, the error recovery process has been considered during the intercluster routing, and security is also accomplished by isolating the malicious nodes by utilizing a sink-based routing example. Mahmoud et al. [12] proposed a new protocol that combines the payment and trust systems with a trust-based and energy-aware routing protocol. The payment system rewards the nodes that relay other packets, and the trust system evaluates the nodes' competence and reliability in relaying packets in terms of multidimensional trust values. Their algorithm stimulates the nodes not only to relay packets but also maintains the route strength and report with sufficient battery power.

Li et al. [13] designed a new routing scheme which provides efficient and fault-tolerant routing. In their work, an evaluation metric and path vacant ratio are used to assess and locate an arrangement of connection disjoint paths from all accessible paths. Moreover, they proposed two more algorithms, namely a congestion control algorithm and load-balancing algorithm. Their congestion control algorithm adjusts the load on multiple paths, and their threshold sharing algorithm splits the packets into multiple segments, which are delivered via multiple paths to the destination using the path vacant ratio in the network. Lee and Choi [14] proposed a secure alternate path routing in sensor network (SeRINS) that detects and isolates the compromised nodes which attempt to infuse conflicting routing information from the system by a neighbor report framework.

Kuila and Jana [32] proposed a new optimized energy-efficient and cluster-based routing algorithm for effective wireless communication. They used a particle swarm optimization algorithm for effective optimization in this work. Mathapati et al. [31] introduced a new cluster and energy-efficient reliable routing algorithm for effective communication in wireless networks. Rahman and Matin [30] developed an algorithm for improving the network lifetime. Younis and Fahmy [29] introduced a new approach called a hybrid, energy-efficient, distributed clustering algorithm for ad-hoc networks. Heinzelman et al. [28] proposed an energy-efficient routing protocol for effective communication. Villas et al. [26] proposed a lightweight and reliable routing technique for aggregating the in-network area in wireless networks. Attea Bara'a [25] introduced an energy-aware routing algorithm for dynamic grouping of wireless networks, which is useful for enhancing the communication process in the network.

Balkis Hamdane et al. [17] explained about security methods based on trust modelling for securing the named date networks. The authors proposed a hierarchical identity-based cryptography for performing signature verification. Their model is providing better performance in terms of key management–based security. Selvi et al. [21] proposed a new fuzzy temporal approach for energy-efficient routing in WSN. Moreover in another work by Selvi et al. [21], the authors proposed a rule-based, delay-constrained, energy-efficient routing technique for wireless sensor networks. However, such approaches must be enhanced with security constraints in order to enhance the security of the routing process. Muthurajkumar et al. [23] proposed an intelligent secured and energy-efficient routing algorithm for MANETs. This work can be extended to both static and mobile sensor networks for providing secured and reliable routing process for WSNs. Idris Abubakar Umar et al. [20] proposed a new security model for performing intelligent secure routing in networks. In their work, the authors used a fuzzy logic–based trust model for handling uncertainty in the trust estimation process and to perform secure routing. In spite of the presence of all these algorithms, the routing performance is affected due to the attackers. Hence, a new trust and energy-aware secure routing protocol is proposed in this chapter.

2.3 System Architecture

Figure 2.1 shows the proposed system architecture. It has seven important components, namely pre-processing phase, clustering

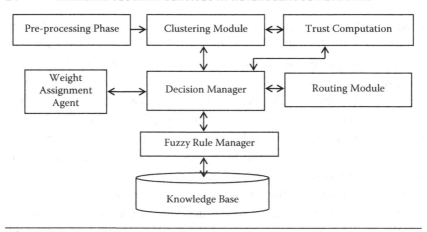

Figure 2.1 System Architecture.

module, fuzzy rule manager, decision manager, knowledge base, trust computation module, weight assignment agent, and routing module. The role of the pre-processing phase in this work is to identify the contributing nodes by selecting the outlier nodes in the network scenario.

The clustering module forms a cluster based on the pre-processing phase recommendation and the energy level of the current nodes. Weighted fuzzy rules are stored in a knowledge base. The fuzzy rule manager communicates with the weight assignment agent for framing fuzzy rules. The decision manager helps to select the suitable nodes for the cluster and cluster head nodes. The trust computation module is responsible for calculating the trust scores for the respective nodes in the dynamic topology. The routing module is responsible for selecting the trust paths with the help of the decision manager's recommendation. The decision manager is responsible for controlling all the components of the proposed system architecture. It makes a decision over the clustering, trust computation, and routing process in the network.

2.4 Proposed Work

The basic system model of the proposed work consists of mobile nodes, which are deployed randomly to monitor an environment. Mobile nodes are homogeneous and have the same initial energy. Mobile nodes are dynamic in nature, and also the energy-constrained and the destination node is equipped with a high energy resource than the participant nodes. The destination node is also located within the network region. The proposed work can be classified into three phases such as pre-processing (outlier selection) phase, clustering phase, trust computation phase, and routing phase. First, outliers are identified in this work based on the weights that are assigned, based on the node energy and distance. Here, outliers are not considered for further processing. Second, new clusters are formed based on the distance and energy. Third, the trust scores for all the nodes which are available in various clusters are calculated. Fourth, the routing process is performed based on the energy level and trust scores of the individual nodes in the network.

2.4.1 Pre-processing

In this section, a FRWDOA for distinguishing the outliers within the network is described. It uses the relative location of some extent with some assigned weight in step with its perceived importance and its neighbor within the feature set to work out the outlier of some extent with regard to all clusters. The overall definitions of weighted distance–based outlier detection as follows: Let f_1, f_2, ..., f_k be the K-nearest neighbors of an object x with weights wt_1, wt_2, wt_3, ..., wt_k. The weighted distance of those k-nearest neighbors is outlined as wt_1ds_1, ws_2ds_2, ..., wt_kds_k where ds_1, ds_2, ..., ds_k are the conventional Minkowski distances $d(x, s_i) = wt_ids_i$. The typical weighted distance is calculated using victimization in (1).

$$\frac{1}{k} * \left(\Sigma_{i=1}^{k} \frac{wt_i \, ds_i}{\Sigma \, wt_i} \right) \tag{1}$$

FRWDOA

The fuzzy rules are framed using the energy level and distance of the nodes and are used for performing the training and testing process for identifying the outliers in the network.

STEP 1: Assign the weighe to the nodes based on the energy level using fuzzy rules.

STEP 2: Calculate the weighted average distance (WAD) for the nodes which are available in the network using (1).

STEP 3: Check whether the nodes of the network distance arebigger than the WAD.

STEP 4: Compute the inner weighted average (IWA) for the k-nearest inner nodes.

STEP 5: Train the nodes which are present in the network to identify the inner and outer nodes.

STEP 6: Compute the weighted distance for a new arriving node using the weights.

STEP 7: If the range (Newly_Arrived_Node) > WAD then

   Add the new node to Non_Outlier_Node_Set
   Else
   Add the new node to Outlier_Node_Set

STEP 8: Stop

Outliers can be identified at the end of this pre-processing stage in this work. The outliers will not be considered for further processing here.

2.4.2 Clustering

This section explains in detail the cluster formation, cluster head selection, cluster maintenance, mobility, and clustering process.

2.4.2.1 Cluster Formation   Initially each node is assigned a random number for identifying it. It proclaims its identity number according to its distance between the neighbor nodes and builds a table which shows the relationship between the nodes in a network. Each participated node calculates its own weights based on node connectivity, energy level, mobility, and distance. Then each node weight is announced to their neighbors after finalizing the weight. The clusters are formed based on the weights, and the node that has the maximum weight acts as a cluster head.

2.4.2.2 Mobility   The mobility of the nodes which are available in the network is measured based on the movement from one place to another in the same topology of the network for a particular time period.

2.4.2.3 Cluster Maintenance Cluster maintenance is needed when a node moves out of the range of its cluster head (CH), if a new node is added or the CH fails. Suppose a new node is added—it computes its weight. However, even if its weight is more than the weight of the CH, it does not immediately become the CH and instead chooses the current CH as its CH. This could reduce the overhead incurred, unnecessarily, every time during the selection of CH while adding a new node. If the CH fails, then the nodes attached to that CH recalculate their weights and select a new node as CH that has the maximum weight.

2.4.2.4 Cluster-Head Selection The CH is selected based on the current energy level of the node and the mobility speed. These two factors are very important for choosing the CH, with consideration of the distance between this node and other neighbor nodes. Here, the node that is closer to the majority nodes with less mobility will be elected as a CH for the cluster.

2.4.2.5 Trust Score Calculation The trust scores are calculated for all the participating nodes in the network. Here, direct, indirect, and reputation scores are considered for calculating the trust score of each node in the network. The direct trust score is calculated using the formula:

$$DTS\ (t1, t2) = PS\ (t1, t2)/ACKR\ (t1, t2) \qquad (2)$$

where PS indicates the number of packets sent and ACKR represents the number of acknowledgements received. Calculate the average direct trust score (AvgDTS) for the whole network by using equation 3.

$$AvgDTS\ (t1, t2) = Sum\ (DTS\ <t1, t2>)/n \qquad (3)$$

where n is the total number of participating nodes in the network at a particular time duration.

The indirect trust scores (IDTS) are calculated for all the nodes in the network using the recommendation score received from neighbor nodes for the particular node.

$$IDTS\ (t1, t2) = (RS1(t1, t2) + RS2(t1, t2) + ...$$
$$+ RSn\ (t1, t2))/n \qquad (4)$$

where RS indicates the recommendation score and n represents the number of recommendations received from neighbor nodes. The average IDTS is calculated for the network using equation 5.

$$\text{AvgIDTS (t1, t2)} = (\text{IDTS}_1 <t1, \ t2> + \text{IDTS}_2 <t1, \ t2> +$$

$$.....+ \text{IDTS} <t1, \ t2>)/n \qquad (5)$$

where n indicate the total number of nodes available in the network.

2.4.2.6 Rules   In this work, IF...THEN rules are framed by using the direct trust, indirect trust, energy, and mobility for identifying the eligible node to participate in the routing process.

Rule 1:

If (DTS_i (t1, t2) < AvgDTS) AND
   (DTS_i (t1, t2) < AvgIDTS) AND
   (Mob_i (t1, t2) < AvgMob) AND
   (En_i (t1, t2) < AvgEn) Then

Node is LOW & Not Eligible to participate in the routing process.

Rule 2:

If (DTS_i (t1, t2) > AvgDTS) AND
   (IDTS_i (t1, t2) > AvgIDTS) AND
   (Mob_i (t1, t2) < AvgMob) AND
   (En_i (t1, t2) < AvgEn) Then

Node is LOW MEDIUM & Eligible to participate in the routing process.

Rule 3:

If (DTS_i (t1, t2) > AvgDTS) AND
   (IDTS_i (t1, t2) > AvgIDTS) AND
   (Mob_i (t1, t2) > AvgMob) AND
   (En_i (t1, t2) > AvgEn) Then

Node is MEDIUM & Eligible to participate in the routing process.

Rule 4:

If (DTS_i (t1, t2) > AvgDTS) AND
   (IDTS_i (t1, t2) > AvgIDTS) AND
   (Mob_i (t1, t2) < AvgMob) AND
   (En_i (t1, t2) > AvgEn) Then

Node is HIGH & Eligible to participate in the routing process and act as CH.

2.4.2.7 Energy Model In this work, the energy model used is similar to the works presented in [24] and [25]. The transmission energy is needed for an l-bit message more than a distance d as per the following (1)

$$E_T(l, d) = \begin{cases} l\ E_{elec} + l\ \varepsilon_{fs}d^2 & for\ d < d_0 \\ l\ E_{elec} + l\ \varepsilon_{mp}d^4 & for\ d \geq d_0 \end{cases} \tag{6}$$

where $d_0 = \sqrt{\varepsilon_{fs}/\varepsilon_{mp}}$

The reception energy required for an l-bit message is given in equation (7).

$$E_R(l) = l\ E_{elec} \tag{7}$$

where E_{elec} – electronic energy

ε_{fs} – amplifier energy in free space and

ε_{mp} – amplifier energy in multipath.

2.4.2.8 Cluster-Based Routing Algorithm In this section, a new cluster-based secure routing algorithm called IWFCSRA has been developed for effective routing in this work. The steps of the proposed algorithm are as follows:

STEP 1: Let DTS = 0, IDTS = 0;

STEP 2: Each node communicates with neighbor nodes to know the DTS at particular time interval.

STEP 3: Source node broadcasts requests to its neighboring nodes. The simulation timer is started.

STEP 4: All nodes receive the request from their neighbors and check whether it is the right destination or not. If it is, an acknowledgement is sent to its neighboring nodes.

STEP 5: Calculate the DTS for all the nodes using the formula

$$DTS\ (t_1, t_2) = PS\ (t_1, t_2)/ACKR\ (t_1, t_2)$$

STEP 6: Calculate the AvgDTS for the network using the formula

$$AvgDTS\ (t_1, t_2) = Sum\ (DTS{<}t_1, t_2{>})/n$$

STEP 7: Calculate the IDTS for all the nodes using the formula

$$\text{IDTS } (t_1, t_2) = (RS_1(t_1, t_2) + RS_2(t_1, t_2) + \dots + RS_n (t_1, t_2))/n$$

STEP 8: Find the AvgIDTS for the network using the formula

$$\text{AvgIDTS } (t_1, t_2) = (\text{IDTS}_1 {<} t_1, t_2 {>} + \text{IDTS}_2 {<} t_1, t_2 {>} + \dots + \text{IDTS}{<} t_1, t_2 {>})/n$$

STEP 9: Apply fuzzy rules to know the normal and malicious nodes

STEP 10: Call a weighted fuzzy C means clustering algorithm [22] for performing a cluster operation.

STEP 11: Finally, detect all the malicious nodes from the network scenario.

STEP 12: Form clusters with normal nodes and perform CH election by applying fuzzy rules, which are framed already for CH selection.

STEP 13: Route the packets through CHs.

2.5 Results and Discussions

The proposed work has been implemented using the simulation tool NS2. The simulation parameters used in this work are given in Table 2.1. The mobile nodes are randomly deployed over a region of 500×500 m^2. The mobile nodes varying from 10 to 100 are deployed with the initial energy of 0.5J. The proposed algorithms are evaluated, and these performances are compared

Table 2.1 Simulation Parameters

PARAMETER	VALUE
Area	500×500 m^2
Sensor Nodes	100
Initial energy	0.5J
E_{elec}	50 nJ/bit
ε_{fs}	10 pJ/bit/m^2
ε_{mp}	0.0013 pJ/bit/m^4
Packet size	4000 bits
Routing Protocol	AODV

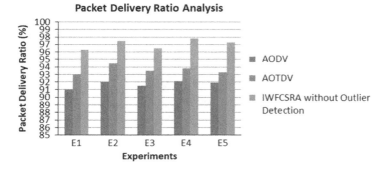

Figure 2.2 Packet Delivery Ratio Analysis Without Outlier Detection.

with the existing algorithms which are proposed in this direction in the past. The comparison is also made with the existing trust-based secure routing algorithms and without trust-based secure routing algorithms.

Figure 2.2 shows the performance of the proposed IWFCSRA without outlier detection. Here, the standard ad-hoc on-demand distance vector (AODV) routing algorithm uses a trust mechanism called the AOTDV algorithm and AODV without a trust model with respect to packet delivery ratio. Here, five experiments such as E1, E2, E3, E4, and E5 have been conducted for evaluating the performance of the proposed system in the particular time period.

From Figure 2.2, it can be observed that the performance of the proposed model without clustering performs better when it is compared with the existing algorithms such as AODV and AOTDV. This is due to the fact that the proposed algorithm uses only the trusted nodes, which are identified by the proposed outlier detection method for effective communication in the network for the particular time period.

The end-to-end delay analysis between the existing routing algorithms, namely AODV and AOTDV and the proposed IWFCSRA without outlier detction, is shown in Figure 2.3. The various experiments have been conducted for measuring the performance of the proposed model.

From Figure 2.3, it can be seen that the use of trust scores to identify the genuine nodes and to perform the routing process through the identified genuine nodes reduces the end-to-end delay when it is compared with the routing process using AODV and AOTDV. The reason for this significant performance improvement is to avoid the

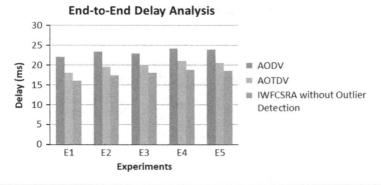

Figure 2.3 End-to-End Delay Analysis.

malicious nodes for the routing process. Moreover, the end-to-end delay is created by malicious nodes, which are avoided by the proposed model.

The packet delivery ratio analysis is shown in Figure 2.4, which considered the proposed model and the existing routing protocols such as AODV, AOTDV, and the proposed IWFCSRA without outlier detection for the analysis. Five different experiments have been conducted for this packet delivery ratio.

From Figure 2.4, it can be seen that the use of the DTS and IDTS improved the packet delivery ratio when compared to the existing secure routing algorithms which use a trust mechanism and clustering technique for making clusters in the network.

Figure 2.5 shows the delay analysis between the standard AODV, AOTDV, AOTDV with clustering, CEESRA, EFCSRA, and the proposed model with trust and clustering.

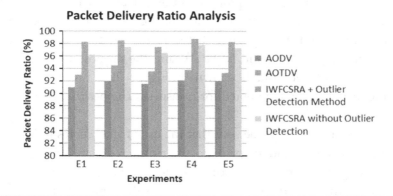

Figure 2.4 Packet Delivery Ratio Analysis.

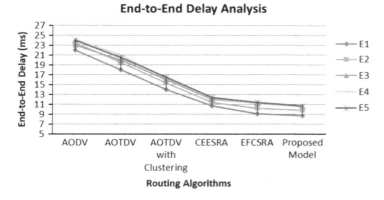

Figure 2.5 End-to-End Delay Analysis Between The Proposed And Existing Works.

From Figure 2.5, it can be seen that the performance of the proposed model is better when it is compared with the existing works such as AODV, AOTDV, AOTDV with clustering, CEESRA, and EFCSRA. The reason for this achievement is the use of fuzzy rules, effective trust computation, and the consideration of energy and mobility for a decision-making process over the malicious nodes.

Figure 2.6 shows the packet delivery ratio analysis between the exisiting algorithms such as AODV, trust-based AODV, cluster- and trust-based secure routing algorithm, and the proposed model. Here, five different mobility speeds from 10 m/s to 50 m/s have been considered for conducting five experiments in this work.

From Figure 2.6, it can be seen that the performance of the proposed model is better than the existing routing algorithms, namely AODV, AOTDV, CEESRA [23], and energy-efficient trust and EFCSRA. This is due to the use of effective fuzzy rules, a new trust mechanism, and the efficient fuzzy C-means clustering technique.

Figure 2.7 shows the energy consumption analysis between the proposed algorithm and the existing routing algorithms such as AODV, AOTDV, CEESRA, and EFCSRA. Here, five different experiments have been conducted by considering five different mobility speeds.

From Figure 2.7, it can be seen that the energy consumption of the proposed IWFCSRA is less when it is compared with the existing routing algorithms such as AODV, AOTDV, CEESRA, and EFCSRA. This is due to the use of effective fuzzy rules and trust mechanism.

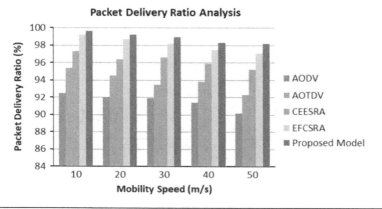

Figure 2.6 Performance Comparative Analysis.

Figure 2.8 shows the security level analysis for the proposed IWFCSRA and the existing routing algorithms such as AODV, AOTDV, CEESRA, and EFCSRA. Here, five experiments have been conducted with different numbers of nodes in the network scenario such as 100, 200, 300, 400, and 500 for analyzing the security level of the proposed work.

From Figure 2.8, it can be observed that the performance of the proposed IWFCSRA is high when it is compared with the existing routing algorithms such as AODV, AOTDV, CEESRA, and EFCSRA. This is due to the use of outlier detection, intelligent fuzzy rules, effective trust mechanism, and the consideration of mobility and energy during the decision-making process over the routing process. The proposed intelligent weighted fuzzy cluster–based secure routing

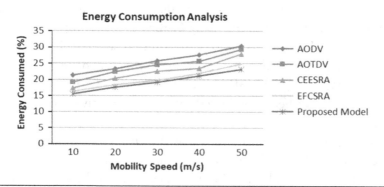

Figure 2.7 Energy Consumption Analysis Under Various Mobility Speeds.

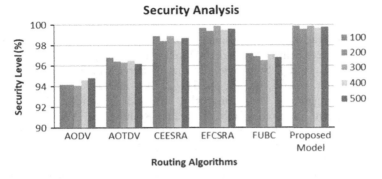

Figure 2.8 Security Level Analysis.

algorithm is evaluated by using various performance metrics such as end-to-end delay, energy consumption, packet delivery ratio, and security level. The overall performance of this proposed work is significantly improved when it is compared with existing works in different evaluation methods.

2.6 Conclusion

In this chapter, an IWFCSRA is proposed in this chapter for MANETs for enhancing the network lifetime and throughputs with security. Moreover, a FRWDOA for distinguishing the outliers within the network is presented. In this proposed work, new fuzzy rules have been generated with weights and used for forming clusters and also used for calculating the trust scores, which are useful for making the final decision over the routing process. Moreover, the final trust paths for the respective clusters have been finalized based on the trust scores, energy, and weighted fuzzy rules in MANETs. From the experiments conducted in this work, it has been seen that our proposed algorithm provides better performance in terms of throughput, delay, and packet transmission compared to the existing algorithms. The main advantages of the proposed secure routing algorithm are the change in the cluster formation with the genuine nodes, increase in malicious node detection accuracy, removal of malicious nodes, and improvement in the routing performance. Future work in this direction could be the use of fuzzy logic for trust score assessment and to improve the decision process in routing under conditions of uncertainty.

References

1. Logambigai, R., and A. Kannan, "Fuzzy Logic Based Unequal Clustering for Wireless Sensor Networks." Wireless Networks, pp. 1–13, 2015.
2. Wood A., and J. Stankovic, "Denial of Service in Sensor Networks." Computer, vol. 35, no. 10, pp. 54–62, Oct. 2002.
3. Kulothungan K., S. Ganapathy, S. Indra Gandhi, P. Yogesh, "Intelligent Secured Fault Tolerant Routing in Wireless Sensor Networks using Clustering Approach." International Journal of Soft Computing, vol. 6, no. 5, pp. 210–215, 2011.
4. Ganapathy S., K. Kulothungan, S. Muthuraj Kumar, M. Vijayalakshmi, "Intelligent Feature Selection and Classification Techniques for Intrusion Detection in Networks: A Survey." EURASIP Journal on Wireless Communication and Networking, vol. 271, no. 1, pp. 1–16, 2013.
5. Guoxing, Zhan, Weisong Shi, and Julia Deng. "Design and Implementation of TARF: A Trust-aware Routing Framework for WSNs." IEEE Transactions on Dependable and Secure Computing, vol. 9, no. 2, pp. 184–197, 2012.
6. Thippeswamy, B. M., S. Reshma, V. Tejaswi, K. Shaila, K. R. Venugopal, and L. M. Patnaik. "STEAR: Secure Trust-Aware Energy-Efficient Adaptive Routing in Wireless Sensor Networks." Journal of Advances in Computer Networks, vol. 3, no. 2, pp. 146–149, 2015.
7. Duan, Junqi, Dong Yang, Haoqing Zhu, Sidong Zhang, and Jing Zhao. "TSRF: A Trust-aware Secure Routing Framework in Wireless Sensor Networks." International Journal of Distributed Sensor Networks, vol. 2014, no. 3, pp. 1–14, 2014.
8. Gu, Wenjun, Neelanjana Dutta, Sriram Chellappan, and Xiaole Bai. "Providing End-to-End Secure Communications in Wireless Sensor Networks." IEEE Transactions on Network and Service Management, vol. 8, no. 3, pp. 205–218, 2011.
9. Tang, Di, Tongtong Li, Jian Ren, and Jie Wu. "Cost-Aware SEcure Routing (CASER) Protocol Design for Wireless Sensor Networks." IEEE Transactions on Parallel and Distributed Systems, vol. 26, no. 4, pp. 960–973, 2015.
10. Souza, Robert John D., and Golla Varaprasad. "Digital Signature-based Secure Node Disjoint Multipath Routing Protocol For Wireless Sensor Networks." IEEE Transactions on Sensors Journal, vol. 12, no. 10, pp. 2941–2949, 2012.
11. Ganesh, Subramanian, and Ramachandran Amutha. "Efficient and Secure Routing Protocol for Wireless Sensor Networks through SNR Based Dynamic Clustering Mechanisms." Journal of Communications and Networks, vol. 15, no. 4, pp. 422–429, 2013.
12. Mahmoud, Mohamed M. E., Xiaodong Lin, and Xuemin Shen. "Secure and Reliable Routing Protocols for Heterogeneous Multihop Wireless Networks." IEEE Transactions on Parallel and Distributed Systems, vol. 26, no. 4, pp. 1140–1153, 2015.

14. Lee, Suk-Bok, and Yoon-Hwa Choi. "A Secure Alternate Path Routing in Sensor Networks." *Computer Communications*, vol. 30, no. 1, pp. 153–165, 2006.
13. Li, Shancang, Shanshan Zhao, Xinheng Wang, Kewang Zhang, and Ling Li. "Adaptive and Secure Load-balancing Routing Protocol for Service-oriented Wireless Sensor Networks." *IEEE Systems Journal*, vol. 8, no. 3, pp. 858–867, 2014.
15. Jaisankar, N., S. Ganapathy, P. Yogesh, A. Kannan, K. Anand, "An Intelligent Agent Based Intrusion Detection System Using Fuzzy Rough Set Based Outlier Detection." Soft Computing Techniques in Vision Science, vol. 395, pp. 147–153, 2012.
16. Ganapathy, S., N. Jaisankar, P. Yogesh, A. Kannan, "An Intelligent System for Intrusion Detection Using Outlier Detection." 2011 International Conference on Recent Trends in Information Technology (ICRTIT), pp. 119–123, 2011.
17. Hamdane, Balkis, Rihab Boussada, Mohamed Elhoucine Elhdhili, Sihem Guemara El Fatmi, "Hierarchical Identity Based Cryptography for Security and Trust in Named Data Networking." 2017 IEEE 26th International Conference on Enabling Technologies: Infrastructure for Collaborative Enterprises, pp. 226–231, 2017.
18. Sethukkarasi, R., S. Ganapathy, P. Yogesh, A. Kannan, "An Intelligent Neuro Fuzzy Temporal Knowledge Representation Model for Mining Temporal Patterns." Journal of Intelligent & Fuzzy Systems, vol. 26, no. 3, pp. 1167–1178, 2014.
19. Ganapathy, S., N. Jaisankar, P. Yogesh, A. Kannan, "An intelligent intrusion detection system using outlier detection and multiclass SVM." International Journal on Recent Trends in Engineering & Technology, vol. 5, no. 1, pp. 166–169, 2011.
20. Umar, Idris Abubakar, Zurina Mohd Hanapi, Aduwati Sali, Zuriati Ahmad Zukarnain, "TruFiX: A Configurable Trust-Based Cross-Layer Protocol for Wireless Sensor Networks." IEEE Access, vol. 5, pp. 2550–2562, 2017.
21. Selvi, M., R. Logambigai, S. Ganapathy, L. S. Ramesh, H. K. Nehemiah, A. Kannan, "Fuzzy Temporal Approach for Energy Efficient Routing in WSN." Proceedings of the International Conference on Informatics and Analytics, pp. 117–122, 2016.
22. Hung, Chih-Cheng, Sameer Kulkarni, Bor-Chen Kuo, "A New Weighted Fuzzy C-Means Clustering Algorithm for Remotely Sensed Image Classification." IEEE Journal of Selected Topics in Signal Processing, vol. 5, no. 3, pp. 543–553, June 2011.
23. Muthurajkumar, S., S. Ganapathy, M. Vijayalakshmi, A. Kannan, "An Intelligent Secured and Energy Efficient Routing Algorithm for MANETs." Wireless Personal Communications, vol. 96, no. 2, pp. 1753–1769, 2017.
24. Selvi, M., P. Velvizhy, S. Ganapathy, H. K. Nehemiah, A. Kannan, "A Rule Based Delay Constrained Energy Efficient Routing Technique for Wireless Sensor Networks." Cluster Computing 22 no. 5, pp. 1–10.

25. Bara'a, A. Attea, "Energy-Aware Evolutionary Routing Protocol for Dynamic Clustering of Wireless Sensor Networks." *Swarm and Evolutionary Computation*, vol. 1, no. 4, pp. 195–203, 2011.

26. Villas, L. A., A. Boukerche, H. S. Ramos, H. A. B. F. de Oliveira, R. B. de Araujo; A. A. F. Loureiro, "DRINA: A Lightweight and Reliable Routing Approach for In-Network Aggregation in Wireless Sensor Networks." IEEE Trans. Computers, vol. 62, no. 4, pp. 676–689, 2013.

27. Nakamura, E. F., H. A. B. F. de Oliveira, L. F. Pontello, and A. A. F. Lourerio, "On Demand Role Assignment for Event Detection in Sensor Networks." 11th Symp, Computers and Comm. (ISCC '06), Sardinia, Italy, pp. 941–947, 2006.

28. Heinzelman, Wendi Rabiner, Anantha Chandrakasan, and Hari Balakrishnan. "Energy-Efficient Communication Protocol for Wireless Microsensor Networks." Annual Hawaii International Conference, System Sciences, pp. 10, 2010.

29. Younis, O., and S. Fahmy, "HEED: A Hybrid, Energy-efficient, Distributed Clustering Approach for Ad Hoc Sensor Networks." IEEE Trans, Mobile Computing, vol. 3, no. 4, pp. 366–379, 2004.

30. Wang, Chu-Fu, Suh-Chien Hang, "Efficient Algorithm for Prolonging Network Lifetime of Wireless Sensor Network." In 2008 Eighth International Conference on Intelligent Systems Design and Applications, vol. 2, pp. 196–201, 2008.

31. Mathapati, Basavaraj S., Siddarama R. Patil, V. D. Mytri, "A Cluster Based Energy Efficient Reliable Routing Protocol for Wireless Sensor Networks." Proc. 1st International Conference, ET2ECN, pp. 1–6, 2012.

32. Kuila, Pratyay, Prasanta K. Jana, "Energy Efficient Clustering And Routing Algorithms For Wireless Sensor Networks: Particle Swarm Optimization Approach." Engineering Applications of Artificial Intelligence, vol. 33, pp. 127–140, 2014.

3

ENSURING SECURITY THROUGH TRUST IN MOBILE AD-HOC NETWORKS USING SOFT COMPUTING METHODS

NAGESWARARAO SIRISALA AND C. SHOBA BINDU

Associate Professor, CSE Dept,
Vardhaman College of Engg,
Hyderabad, India
Professor, CSE Dept, JNTUACE,
Anantapur, India

Contents

3.1 Introduction

In mobile ad-hoc networks(MANETs), a node has to interact with unknown nodes in establishing the network. The applications are run successfully, if all the nodes are cooperative. Hence, the trust computation of each node is certainly an advantage in running applications effectively by eliminating untrustworthy nodes. Due to the severe resource constrains (like energy, computational power, bandwidth, and time) and dynamics (like topological changes, mobility, and channel conditions) of the network, creation of a secure environment by implementing complex encryption algorithms (hard security) is not a trivial task [8]. Alternatively, researchers have concentrated on soft security (trust) methods to separate malicious nodes by monitoring their activities.

In MANET, usually a node switches to selfish mode when it is short of resources, and it may not cooperate in running neighbor applications. Due to malicious behavior, a node can weaken the network performance by dropping or tampering with packets. In this regard, authors [1,2] suggest taking into account a node's ability (in terms of resources) and attitude in its trust estimation. Through the node trust computation, the quality of service (QoS) of the applications in the network can be improved [10,12].

In this chapter in Section 2, trust definitions, properties, prediction, aggregation, propagation, and computation methods are discussed in the MANET context. Different trust attacks in MANETs and their countermeasures are discussed in Section 3. In Section 4, soft computing methods in trust estimation are discussed like fuzzy logic, fuzzy petrinets, Bayesian conditional probability, Dempsters Shafer Theory (DST), and trust matrix operations.

3.2 Trust in Mobile Ad-hoc Networks

Trust is platform independent, and the principles of trust are even applicable to the communication network. In current research, trust is being considered as one of the design considerations in a networking protocol stack [4]. In the distributed environment of MANETs, maintenance of trust relations with other nodes can increase the network performance like scalability, dependability, and reliability. In this section, these concepts are discussed in the MANET context.

3.2.1 Trust Definitions

The term "trust" is defined in multiple ways, but the widely accepted two definitions are discussed here.

In [14], the trust of a particular node is a subjective assessment by an agent/other peer node on the reliability and accuracy of information received from or traversing through that node in a given context.

In [13], trust reflects the belief or confidence or expectations in terms of the honesty, integrity, ability, availability, and quality of service of a target node's future activity/behavior. It also reflects the mutual relationships where a given node behaves in a trustworthy manner and maintains reliable communications only with nodes that are highly trusted by the given node.

3.2.2 Trust Properties in MANETs

In Figure 3.1, the trust properties are described from a MANET perspective, where the trust is shown as the combination of properties like asymmetry, subjectivity, context dependency, dynamicity, and transitivity.

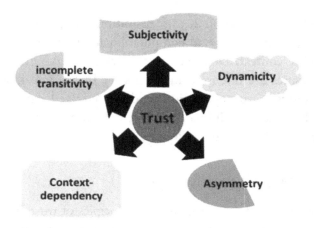

Figure 3.1 Trust Properties in MANETs.

Trust is dynamic: In MANETs, node behavior is not static; it changes based on conditions over time. Hence, the node's trust is a variable factor. In [15], Adams et al. recommended a random variable to capture the trust changes instead of a discrete variable.

Trust is subjective: In a network, a node can have different opinions on other nodes at different time intervals, where these trust changes are influenced by the network topology conditions.

Trust is asymmetric: Usually ad-hoc networks are formed with the heterogeneous nodes, where nodes have different capabilities like computational power, memory, battery power, etc. Hence, the trust relation between two nodes is not symmetric. Generally, a node with good resources has good trust with its neighbors.

Trust is transitive: A node can assess the trustworthiness of a target node through intermediate nodes using a trust transitivity rule. Let us consider three nodes (n_i, n_j, n_k), where n_j is the neighbor of both n_i and n_k, but n_i and n_k are not neighbors. Node n_i takes the trust recommendation of n_j to estimate the trustworthiness of n_k.

Trust is context dependent: In ad-hoc networks, trust is context dependent, i.e. a node has different trust opinions of the same node in different contexts. A node can trust another node in an energy context but cannot trust in a bandwidth context, for example.

3.2.3 Trust Propagation

The computed trust values have to be shared among the nodes in the network, so that the trust recomputation works can be avoided for the same node. For this each node exchange trusts information with its neighbour nodes.

3.2.4 Trust Aggregation

Sometimes a node may receive multiple trust recommendations through multiple channels about the target node. But the assessor node has to combine these values to derive a single trust value. The aggregation functions play a major role in trust aggregation, where they can eliminate or suppress biased trust recommendations. Let a node receive multiple trust values from different sources like x_1, x_2, ... x_n, the aggregate function produces the single trust value.

$$y = Aggre\ (x_1,\ x_2,\ ..... \ x_n)$$

3.2.5 Trust Prediction

If a node cannot asses a target node trust value either directly or indirectly, it has to predict the trust value. A node can predict the trust value based on its present and past interactions with the target node.

3.2.6 Trust Computation

In ad-hoc networks, the trust can be computed in three different ways, i.e. direct, indirect, and hybrid trust computation. If the target node is in direct communication, then trust can be computed directly. For the nodes that are not in direct communications, indirect trust is computed. Hybrid is the combination of direct and indirect trust computations.

3.2.6.1 Direct Trust Computation   Usually in MANETs, a node can observes its neighbor nodes' activities due to the broadcast nature of the wireless channel. Hence, a node can estimate its one-hop neighbors' trust values based on control and data packets it exchanged with them.

In [16], the direct trust is evaluated using Equation (1).

$$T = R_P \times W(R_P) + R_q \times W(R_q) + R_e \times W(R_e) + D \times W(D)$$

$$(1)$$

Here D, R_q, R_P, and R_e are misbehavior factors of data packets, route request, route reply, and route error packets, respectively, and are defined in Equation (2) as normalized values [0, 1].

$$R_q = \frac{R_{qs} - R_{qf}}{R_{qs} + R_{qf}} \quad R_{es} = \frac{R_{es} - R_{ef}}{R_{es} + R_{ef}} \quad R_p = \frac{R_{ps} - R_{qf}}{R_{ps} + R_{qf}} \quad D = \frac{D_s - D_f}{D_s + D_f}$$

$$(2)$$

Here R_{qs}, R_{es}, R_{ps}, and D_s are defined as the number of route requests, route error, route reply, and data packets that are successfully forwarded by node B. R_{qf}, R_{ef}, R_{pf}, and D_f are the number of route requests, route error, route reply, and data packets that are not forwarded (failed) by node B. Here $W()$. represents the weights that are given to different packets in the trust calculation.

3.2.6.2 Recommendation-Based Trust   Here c_{ij}. indicates the confidence level of node i of node j, and this value lies in the range of [-1,1]. The confidence parameter is not symmetric. Hence, the confidence level in between node i and j is calculated as an average value of their confidence values on each other using Equation (3).

$$\hat{c}_{ij} = \frac{c_{ij} + c_{ji}}{2}$$

$$(3)$$

$T_i(k)$ is the trust value of node i at k instant of time. $T_i(k + 1)$ is calculated as in Equation (4)

$$T_i(k + 1) = \begin{cases} 1, & m_i(k) > \tau \\ -1, & m_i(k) < \tau \end{cases}$$

$$(4)$$

Here $m_i(k)$. is the trust value of node i based on the recommendations of other nodes. τ is the trust threshold value as in Equation (5).

$$m_i(k) = \sum_{j \in N_i} \hat{c}_{ji} T_j(k) \tag{5}$$

3.2.6.3 Hybrid Method In the hybrid method, a node can evaluate the target node;s trust value based on its direct interactions and by considering other node recommendations. The hybrid trust is computed using Equation (6)

$$T_{a,b} = \alpha T_d + \beta T_r \tag{6}$$

Here T_d and T_r represent direct and recommended trust, respectively. α, β represents weights to the direct and recommended trusts, respectively, where $\alpha + \beta = 1$.

3.3 Trust Distortion Attacks: A Taxonomy

Various trust-based attacks are discussed here. Attacks over trust systems can cause of propagation of wrong trust information in the network and weaken the performance of trust computing methods.

3.3.1 Trust Attacks in MANETs

In Figure 3.2, trust attacks are primarily categorized as badmouthing and double-face attacks [4]. Badmouthing attacks are like liar and subversive. Double-face attacks are like position/user domain, detonator, and iterative attacks.

3.3.1.1 Badmouthing Attacks In [17], badmouthing attacks are discussed, which are also called lying attacks. In a badmouthing attack,

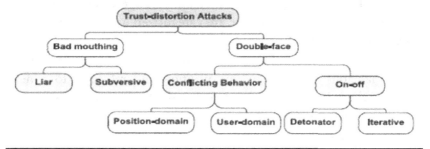

Figure 3.2 Trust Distortion Attacks.

the compromised nodes spread biased trust recommendations in the network, so that the evaluator node cannot estimate the target node trust value accurately. Here, the attacker can show the trustworthy node as a malicious node and vice versa by giving a false recommendation. Usually, the trust components that are dependent on recommendations face these problems. As shown in Figure 3.3, the liar attack is one where the attacker node always gives false recommendations to the assessor node.

In a subversive attack, the attacker performs misbehavior like dropping or modifying packets and propagating false news.

3.3.1.2 Double-Face Attacks   In a double-face attack, the attacker cannot be identified by performing harmful activities at nonregular intervals [4]. The attacker can hide his identity by behaving good and bad at uneven time intervals. The double-face attacks are either on-off or conflicting behavior attacks based on if the threat impact is spatial or temporal.

On-off attack: Here the attacker always maintains the trust value above the threshold level by doing malicious activities at unexpected time intervals. The attacker keeps moving between misbehavior (on) and normal (off) states to hide his identity. The on-off attacks are of two types, i.e. iterative attacks and detonator. In the iterative on-off attack, the attacker iteratively switches good and bad manners to mislead the observer node. In a detonator on-off attack, an attacker in a good manner can create trustworthiness over a certain period of time. After a period, the user can induce malicious activities and continuous in that state fatherly.

Conflicting behavior attack: In this attack, an attacker node shows a different attitude in different positions in the network to remain undetected as a malicious node. Based on the targeted entity (i.e. user or group of users), these attacks are categorized as user domain and position domain attacks.

Position domain conflicting behavior attack: An attacker node performs malicious activities in one position and relocates to a new position where it behaves as a normal node. So it remains as a good node in the new position. Usually these types of attacks can be addressed through the trust propagation throughout the network, so that all nodes come to know the past behavior of new joined nodes.

User domain conflicting behavior attack: An attacker always attacks only a targeted node or group of nodes and remains good with all other nodes. Hence, the victim node cannot get any help from other nodes to oppose the attacker. This situation may lead to isolating the victim node, since it is giving negative feedback about the attacker. These types of attacks can be addressed by taking the recommender node trust value into consideration.

3.3.2 Trust-Distortion Resistant Trust Management Frameworks

To overcome trust attacks like badmouthing and double-face, many trust management frameworks (TMFs) are proposed. Here some of them are discussed.

3.3.2.1 TMFs Resistant to Double-Face Attacks
The following TMFs are intended to address the double-face type of attacks.

Bella: In [19], Bella et al. proposed the framework which works based on local trust information and trust recommendations. Each node collects local trust information of one-hop neighbors through the direct interactions using the knowledge collection component. The framework maintains the global reputation table (GRT) in each node to maintain the trust information of all nodes in the network.

Almotiri: This is proposed in [20]. This TMF is designed to resist double-face attacks in MANETs. Here at each node the knowledge collection component records all successful and unsuccessful communications with one-hop neighbor nodes. Each node will get updated about multihop-away nodes' trust information through the control packets (RREQ, RREP) in the routing process.

3.3.2.2 TMFs Resistant to BadMouthing Attacks
The following methods explain TMSs that resist the badmouthing attacks.

OTMF: The objective trust management framework (OTMF) [22] is proposed in [30]. It can address both double-face and badmouthing attacks. Here both present and past behaviors of a node are considered to estimate its trust value, where present behaviors are given more weight than past behaviors. Additionally, the trust value of the recommender node is also considered.

LARS: A locally aware reputation system (LARS) is proposed in [21], which can address badmouthing and on-off attacks. At each node the knowledge collection component uses the watchdog mechanism in assessing neighbor node behaviour. Here in data transmission, a node sets the timer after sending data to the destination node. If the node does not receive any acknowledgement before timing out, it starts the probe by sending a special trace packet to find the malicious node along the route.

3.4 Trust Management Using Soft Computing Methods in MANETs

In MANETs, the applications run successfully only with the cooperation and coordination of all the nodes in the network. Usually, a node switches to selfish mode when short of resources and will not cooperate with other nodes. Some of the articles [3,5] proposed that the trust computing methods should consider a node attitude and ability (in terms of its available resources) in its trust estimation. These methods can improve the quality of service (QoS) of the applications, since each node's resources (quality parameters) are taken into consideration in the trust computation. Some of the lightweight soft computing methods include the following:

➢ Fuzzy logic
➢ Fuzzy Petri nets
➢ Bayesian conditional probability
➢ Demsters Shafer theory
➢ Trust matrices

3.4.1 Trust Computation Using Fuzzy Logic

In [6], a fuzzy-based QoS trust model is proposed, and it is explained in Figure 3.3. Here the node ability and attitude are considered in the trust computation. Node ability is evaluated in terms of its QoS metrics like link expiry time (LET), bandwidth, and energy, whereas attitude is evaluated in terms of its reliability. Here the fuzzy logic is used to combine all these QoS metrics to derive a node trust value.

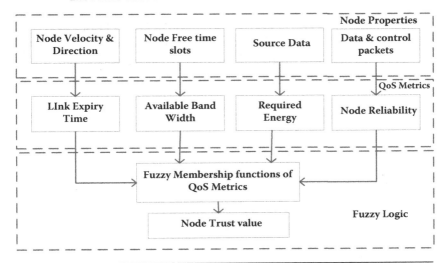

Figure 3.3 Fuzzy inference QoS trust model.

In further sections, first QoS metrics are evaluated and then fuzzy logic (fuzzification, defuzzyfication, and fuzzy rule base) is discussed to compute the trust value.

3.4.1.1 Computation of QoS Parameters In [5], the computation of LET, energy, bandwidth, and reliability is discussed.

Estimation of LET: The LET between two nodes is calculated based on their present locations, velocity, and moving direction. It is estimated using Equation (7).

$$\text{LET} = \frac{-(ab + cd) + \sqrt{(a^2 + c^2)r^2 - (ad - cb)^2}}{(a^2 + c^2)} \tag{7}$$

Table 3.1 LET Notations

$a = v_1 \cos \theta_1 - v_2 \cos \theta_2$

$b = x_1 - x_2$

$c = v_1 \sin \theta_1 - v_2 \sin \theta_2$

$d = y_1 - y_2$

(x_1, y_1) and (x_1, y_1) are node locations

v_1 and v_2 are their velocities

θ_1 and θ_2 are their directions

Node energy calculation: Here, packet-forwarding energy is calculated in Equation (8). In forwarding a packet, a node has to receive and transmit to other nodes. Hence, it is the combination of receiving and transmitting energies.

$$E_{total}(k) = E_{amp} \times k \times d^2 + 2 \times (E_{ele} \times k) \tag{8}$$

Table 3.2   Energy Notations

E_{ele} is the transceiver energy
E_{amp} is the amplifier energy
k is the data size in bits
d is the radio coverage

Bandwidth calculation using TDMA: The time division multiple access (TDMA) is used in bandwidth calculation, where the link bandwidth between two nodes is calculated in terms of their common time slots [13].

In Equation (9), a node n_i can transmit data to neighbor node n_j in time slot s_t, if that time slot is not scheduled at any neighbor of n_i as a receiving slot.

$$TS_i = \{s_t \in S: s_t \notin TS_i, s_t \notin RS_i, s_t \notin \cup_{n_k \in NB_i} RS_k\} \tag{9}$$

In Equation (10), a node n_i can receive data from neighbor node n_j in time slot s_t, if that time slot is not scheduled at any neighbor of n_j as a transmit slot.

$$RS_i = \{s_t \in S: s_t \notin TS_i, s_t \notin RS_i, s_t \notin \cup_{n_k \in NB_i} TS_k\} \tag{10}$$

Node reliability: Node reliability is estimated based on the packet forwarding nature, and it is formulated in Eq. (10). If a node received y total number of packets and among them it forwarded x number of packets, then using Bayesian conditional probability [9], its reliability r is calculated as

$$f(r, y/x) = \frac{P(x/r, y)f(r, y)}{\int_0^1 P(x/r, y)f(r, y)dr} \tag{11}$$

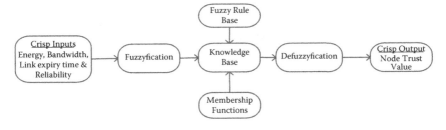

Figure 3.4 Fuzzy Logic in FQTM.

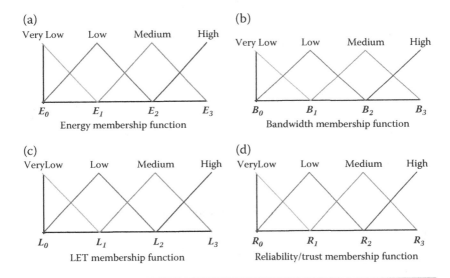

Figure 3.5 Triangular Membership Functions of Fuzzy Input Variables. (a) Energy Membership Function. (b)Bandwidth Membership Function. (c) LET Membership Function. (D) Reliability/trust Membership Function.

3.4.1.2 Fuzzy Inference System to Evaluate Node Trust Values In Figure 3.4, the fuzzy logic [7] is applied in the computation of node trust value, where QoS parameters are considered as fuzzy input parameters and node trust is the fuzzy output.

Fuzzification: In fuzzification, each QoS metric is represented in membership function, where it is quantified as very low, low, medium, or high. In Figure 3.5, QoS memberships are shown.

Table 3.3 Fuzzy Rule Base

ENERGY	LET	BANDWIDTH	RELIABILITY	TRUST
High	High	High	High	High
High	Medium	High	High	High
Medium	Low	Medium	High	Medium
High	Medium	Medium	High	Medium

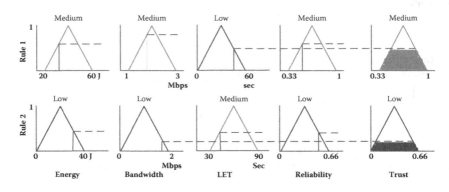

Figure 3.6 Example of Node Trust Evaluation.

Rule base: In the rule base the rules are framed in the form of IF-THEN conditions, which can be used to combine the fuzzy input functions to derive trust value. Some of the sample rules are described in Table 3.3.

Fuzzy inference system:

In Figure 3.6, the QoS parameters are combined using the following rules.

1. Rule 1: If (energy is Medium, Bandwidth is Medium, LET is Low and Reliability is Medium) then (Trust is Medium)
2. Rule 2: If (energy is Low, Bandwidth is Low, LET is Medium and Reliability is Low) then (Trust is Low)

Here the input crisp values of QoS metrics of energy, bandwidth, LET, and reliability are 32J, 1.8 Mbps, 42 sec, and 0.528, respectively.

Defuzzification: In Figure 3.6 the portions of output trust parameters are combined. As shown in Figure 3.7, the center of gravity (COG) method is used to find the trust value using Equation (12).

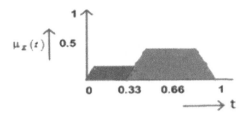

Figure 3.7 Defuzzificaion of Node Trust Value.

$$COG = \frac{\int_0^1 \mu_E\ (t)\ t\ dt}{\int_0^1 \mu_E\ (t)\ dt} \tag{12}$$

3.4.2 Trust Routing Using Fuzzy Petri-Nets in MANETs

Here the routing process is discussed with the help of a dynamic fuzzy Petri-nets (DFPNs) model. In [11], the DFPN is discussed. In Figure 3.8, the DFPN is shown as the graph-related structure and the combination of places and transitions, where places are shown as circles and transitions are shown as bars. A directed arc connects the input place (P_j) to the output place (P_k), and each arc is associated with a transition (t_i). The input place consists of a token with some degree of trust (d_j) (DoT). Each transition is associated with two parameters like (μ, τ); a transition fires if $\mu > \tau$ and the token is moved from the input place to output place with a new DoT (i.e. d_k).

Here the degree of trust of place p_j is d_j i.e. $\propto (p_j) = d_j$. After firing the transition $t_i(\mu > \tau)$, the token is copied from place p_j to p_k. Then the degree of truth for place p_k is evaluated as $d_k = d_j \times w \times \mu$.

3.4.2.1 Weighted Rules of DFPN

In Figure 3.9, the transition has m inputs after firing the transition t_i, $d_k = (d_{j1} \times w_1 + d_{j2} \times w_2 \ldots\ldots d_{jm} \times w_m) \times \mu$.

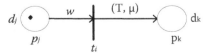

Figure 3.8 DAFPN Representation of Type 1 Rule.

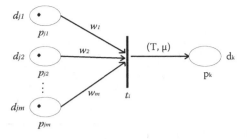

Figure 3.9 DFPN Weighted Rule 1

In Figure 3.10, the transition has multiple outputs; the degree of every output is evaluated as $d_{ki} = d_j \times w \times \mu_i$.

3.4.2.2 MANET Routing Using DFPN Fuzzy-based certainty factor (μ) evaluation: In Figure 3.11, the MANET network is modeled as DFPN, where the places are similar to nodes and the transition is like a wireless link. Here, the certainty factor of transition is evaluated based on a fuzzy system, as explained earlier, by considering the QoS parameters of both nodes (like energy, BW, LET, and reliability). Once the transition fires (nodes have sufficient resources μ > τ), the packet is forwarded from input node to output node. The threshold value (τ) for each transition is calculated based on network conditions.

Fuzzy Petri-net–based routing algorithm:

1. The source node n_s sends the route request (RREQ) to its one-hop neighbors by setting DOT as 1, ∝ (n_s) = 1.
2. Here w = 1 (all are single-input transitions)

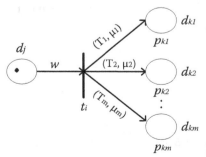

Figure 3.10 DFPN Weighted Rule 1.

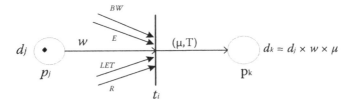

Figure 3.11 CF Computation.

3. After receiving the RREQ packet, each intermediate node evaluates μ. It forwards the RREQ packet if $\mu > \tau$. Otherwise, it drops the request.
4. In traveling, the RREQ packet multiplies the DOTs for all nodes through which it has come across.
5. The destination node accepts the RREQ packet with the highest DOT and gives a reply.

QTFPN routing with an example topology:

In Figure 3.12(a), the example MANET topology is shown with eight nodes, where 1, 8 are source and destination nodes. In Figure 3.12(b), the same MANET is modeled as a DFPN. Here, the source has five alternative paths to the destination node, i.e. 1-2-5-8, 1-3-5-8, 1-3-6-8, 1-4-6-8 and 1-4-7-8. But the route 1-4-6-8 is not valid due to $\mu < \tau$. Next, the DoT value of route 1-2-5-8 is evaluated as.

$$(1 \times 0.8) > 0.3 \Rightarrow 0.8$$
$$(0.8 \times 0.7) > 0.4 \Rightarrow 0.56$$
$$(0.56 \times 0.8) > 0.3 \Rightarrow 0.448$$

Likewise, we can evaluate the DoT values for the remaining three paths as 0.576, 0.567, and 0.448, respectively. Here, the path 1-3-5-8 has the maximum DoT; hence, the destination chooses this path.

3.4.3 Dempster-Shafer Theory

Demspter-Shafer theory [3] is the mathematical aggregation function. A node uses DST to aggregate multiple trust recommendations

(a)

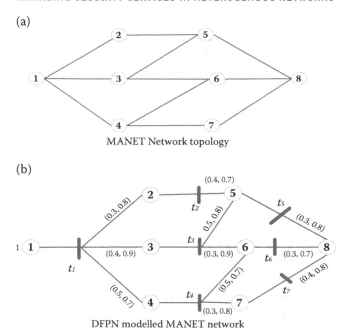

MANET Network topology

(b)

DFPN modelled MANET network

Figure 3.12 (a) MANET Network Topology. (b) DFPN-Modeled MANET Network.

that are received from multiple paths. The DST method can identify the bias recommendations, and it can reduce the impact of biased recommendation in trust computations.

The DST function depends on three functions, i.e. mass function, plausibility function (Pl), and belief function (Bel). Let an event e happen, and $E = \{e_1, e_2, e_3\}$ is the set of evidences about the event e The power set $P(E)$ is the $\{\emptyset, \{e_1\}, \{e_2\}, \{e_3\}\{e_1, e_2\}, \{e_2, e_3\}, \{e_1, e_3\}, \{e_1, e_2, e_3\}\}$.

Mass function: The mass function(m) maps all the subsets in P(E) to the range [0,1], $m:P(E) \rightarrow [01]$ where $m(\emptyset) = 0$ and $\Sigma_{B \in P(E)} m(B) = 1$.

Belief function (Bel): If X is the subset in (E), then $bel(X) = \Sigma_{C \subseteq X} m(C)$.

Plausibility function(pl): If X is the subset in P(E), then $pl(X) = \Sigma_{C \cap X \neq \emptyset} m(C)$.

3.4.3.1 Dempster's Rule for Combinations Let X be the element in

Figure 3.13 Aggregation of QoS Trust Recommendations.

$P(E)$, and A and B are two observer nodes about event X. Their observations are represented as $m_A(X)$, $m_B(X)$. The combination of these two observations can be calculated using Equation (13).

$$m_{A,B}(X) = \frac{\sum_{P \cap Q=X} m_A(P) m_B(Q)}{1 - K} \tag{13}$$

where the constant K is defined as $K = \sum_{P \cap Q=\varnothing} m_A(P) m_B(Q)$.

3.4.3.2 DST Example In Figure 3.13, node S is taking a trust recommendation from nodes P and Q about node D. The trust recommendation is in the form $(T, \overline{T}, U)$, i.e. trust, distrust, and uncertainty, respectively. Here nodes P and Q trust recommendations on node D are {0.7, 0.2, 0.1} and {0.3, 0.5, 0.2}, respectively. These recommendations are multiplied with their trust values.

Node S has 0.9 trust on P, so P's trust is recalculated as

$$m_P(T) = T_P \times 0.7 = 0.63$$
$$m_P(\overline{T}) = T_P \times 0.2 = 0.18$$
$$m_P(U) = T_P \times 0.1 = 0.09$$

Node S has 0.8 trust on P, so Q's trust is recalculated as

$$m_Q(T) = T_Q \times 0.3 = 0.24$$
$$m_Q(\overline{T}) = T_Q \times 0.5 = 0.40$$
$$m_Q(U) = T_Q \times 0.2 = 0.16$$

The aggregation of P,Q node recommendations on node D is evaluated as in Equation (21).

$$m_{P,Q}(T) = \frac{m_P(T)\,m_Q(T) + m_P(T)\,m_Q(U) + m_P(U)\,m_Q(T)}{1 - [m_P(T)\,m_Q(\overline{T}) + m_P(\overline{T})\,m_Q(T)]}$$

$$= \frac{0.05}{0.09} = 0.55$$

This equation can be extended for combining n node recommendations on node D, i.e. $m_{1\ldots n}(T)$.

3.4.4 Trust Matrix Operations

Trust matrix operations are used for propagating trust values in the network to avoid the risk of trust computational work of the same node.

Here each node has the trust information, and it maintains the information in a matrix format of $n \times n$ order (n represents the number of nodes in the network).

$$N^T = \begin{pmatrix} t_{11} & \cdots & t_{k1} & \cdots & t_{n1} \\ \cdots & & & & \cdots \\ t_{1k} & \cdots & t_{kk} & \cdots & t_{nk} \\ \cdots & & & & \cdots \\ t_{1n} & \cdots & t_{kn} & \cdots & t_{nn} \end{pmatrix} \tag{14}$$

In Equation (14), t_{ij} means the node i trust value on node j. Using trust matrix operations, a node can calculate the trust value of a target node that is not in direct communication (by applying a trust transitive rule).

Trust transitive rule:

    i. t_{ij} : node i trust value on node j
    ii. t_{jk}: node j trust value on node k
    iii. Then node i trust value on node k is evaluated as $t_{ik} = t_{ij} * t_{jk}$.

Let $t_i = [t_{i1}\ldots t_{ik}\ldots t_{in}]$ be the trust vector of node i; it can get updated iteratively by using Equation (15).

$$\begin{pmatrix} t_{i1} \\ \cdots \\ t_{ik} \\ \cdots \\ t_{in} \end{pmatrix}_{NEXT} = \begin{pmatrix} t_{11} & \cdots & t_{k1} & \cdots & t_{N1} \\ \cdots & & & & \cdots \\ t_{1k} & \cdots & t_{kk} & \cdots & t_{Nk} \\ \cdots & & & & \cdots \\ t_{1n} & \cdots & t_{kn} & \cdots & t_{nn} \end{pmatrix} \otimes \begin{pmatrix} t_{i1} \\ \cdots \\ t_{ik} \\ \cdots \\ t_{in} \end{pmatrix}_{CURRENT} \tag{15}$$

In Equation 15, the value t_{ik} is evaluated as

$$t_{ik} = max_{1 \leq j \leq n}\{t_{ij} \times t_{jk}\}.$$

Here node i can apply this formula iteratively to find the trust values of multichip away nodes like

$$t_i = (N^T)t_i$$
$$t_i = (N^T)^2 t_i$$
$$\vdots$$
$$t_i = (N^T)^n t_i$$

3.5 Conclusion

In MANETs, due to resource constraints and network dynamics, the implementation of complex security algorithms degrades network performance. In this work, this limitation is overcome with trust handling methods. Here node trust is evaluated by taking into consideration ability (resources) and attitude. A comprehensive discussion was provided on the trust attacks and their countermeasures. Different soft computing techniques (i.e. fuzzy logic, fuzzy Petrinets, Dempster-Shafer theory, and trust matrix operations) are discussed for trust management in MANETs.

References

1. NageswaraRao Sirisala and C. Shoba Bindu. A Novel QoS Trust Computation in MANETs Using Fuzzy Petri Nets, International Journal of Intelligent Engineering and Systems, vol. 10, no. 2, 2017, pp. 116–125.
2. Yating Wang; Ing-Ray Chen;Trust-Based Task Assignment With Multiobjective Optimization in Service-Oriented Ad Hoc Networks, vol. 14, no. 1, 2017, pp. 217–232.
3. NageswaraRao Sirisala and C.Shoba Bindu. Recommendations Based QoS Trust Aggregation and Routing in Mobile Adhoc Networks, International Journal of Communication Networks and Information Security (IJCNIS), vol. 8, no. 3, 2016, pp. 215–220.
4. Zeinab Movahedi, Zahra Hosseini Trust-Distortion Resistant Trust Management Frameworks on Mobile Ad Hoc Networks: A Survey, IEEE Communications Surveys & Tutorials, vol. 18, no. 2, 2016, pp. 1287–1309.
5. NageswaraRao Sirisala and C.Shoba Bindu. Fuzzy Based Quality of Service Trust Model for Multicast Routing in Mobile Adhoc Networks, International Journal of Applied Engineering Research vol. 10, no. 12, 2015, pp. 32175–32194.
6. NageswaraRao Sirisala and C. Shoba Bindu. Uncertain Rule Based Fuzzy Logic QoS Trust Model in MANETs, *International Conference on Advanced Computing and Communications -ADCOM, (IITM PhD forum)*, 2015, pp. 55–60.
7. F. Hao, G. Min and M.Lin. MobiFuzzyTrust: An Efficient Fuzzy Trust Inference Mechanism in Mobile Social Networks, IEEE Transactions on Parallel and Distributed Systems, vol. 25, no. 11, 2014 pp. 2944–2955.
8. NageswaraRao Sirisala and C.Shoba Bindu. Weightage Based Trusted QoS Protocol in Mobile Adhoc Networks, *IEEE Global Conference on Wireless Computing and Networking*, 2014, pp. 283–287.
9. W. Zhexiong, and Tang. Security Enhancements for Mobile Ad Hoc Networks With Trust Management Using Uncertain Reasoning, IEEE Transactions on Vehicular Technology, vol. 63, no. 9, 2014 pp. 4647–4658.
10. F. Bao, J. Hee and C. Ing-Ray. Trust Management in Mobile Ad Hoc Networks for Bias Minimization and Application Performance Maximization, Ad Hoc Networks, vol. 19, 2014 pp. 59–74.
11. H. C. Liu, and L. Liu, Knowledge Acquisition and Representation Using Fuzzy Evidential Reasoning and Dynamic Adaptive Fuzzy Petri Nets, IEEE Transactions On Cybernetics, vol. 43, no. 3, 2013, pp. 1059–1072.
12. Lei Ju, Edwin H. M. Sha, Hui Xia, Zhiping Jia, Xin Li, Trust Prediction and Trust-based Source Routing in Mobile Ad Hoc Networks Ad Hoc Networks Elsevier, vol. 11, no. 7, 2013, pp. 2096–2114.

13. C.C. Hu, H. Wu, and G.H. Chen, Bandwidth-Satisfied Multicast Trees in MANETs, *IEEE Transactions On Mobile Computing*, vol. 7, no. 6, 2008, pp. 712–723.
14. P. Mohapatra and K. Govindan. Trust Computations and Trust Dynamics in Mobile Adhoc Networks: A Survey, IEEE Communications Surveys and Tutorials, vol. 14, no. 2, 2012, pp. 279–298.
15. J.-H. Cho, A. Swami, and I.-R. Chen, A Survey on Trust Management for Mobile Ad Hoc Networks, IEEE Communications Surveys Tutorials, vol. 13, no. 4, Nov. 2011, pp. 562–583.
16. W. J. Adams, G. C. Hadjichristofi and N. J. Davis, Calculating a Node's Reputation in a Mobile Ad Hoc Network, Proceedings of 24th IEEE International Performance Computing and Communications Conference, Phoenix, AX, 7–9 April 2005, pp. 303–307.
17. Pirzada and C. McDonald. Trust Establishment in Pure Ad-Hoc Networks, International Journal of Wireless Personal Communications, vol. 37, 2006, pp. 139–168
18. P. B. Velloso, R. P. Laufer, D. O. Cunha, O. C. M. B. Duarte, and G. Pujolle, Trust Management in Mobile Ad Hoc Networks Using a Scalable Maturity-based Model, IEEE Transactions on Network and Service Management, vol. 7, no. 3, Sep. 2010, pp. 172–185.
19. G. Bella, G. Costantino, and S. Riccobene, Managing Reputation Over MANETS, in Proceedings of 4th International Conference on Information Assurance Security (IAS), 2008, pp. 255–260.
20. S. Almotiri and I. Awan, Trust Routing in MANET for Securing DSR Routing Protocol, PGNet, 2010.
21. J. Hu and M. Burmester, Cooperation in Mobile Ad Hoc Networks, in Proceedings of Guide to Wireless Ad Hoc Networks, 2009, pp. 43–57.
22. J. Li, R. Li, and J. Kato, Future Trust Management Framework For Mobile Ad Hoc Networks, IEEE Communications Magazine, vol. 46, no. 4, Apr. 2008, pp. 108–114.

4

PROOF OF VIRTUE: NONCE-FREE HASH GENERATION IN BLOCKCHAIN

J. JAYAPRIYA AND N. JEYANTHI

School of Information Technology and Engineering, VIT, Vellore, India

Contents

Highlights

1. Computational and other energy resource waste is brought down due to the removal of nonce (puzzle) generation in the hash generation process.
2. Mining power does not play any role in block generation, which prevents 51% of attacks.
3. A new user has to wait for a certain period until he gets the

required credit score for participating in the block generation process, which will make the network Sybil resistant.

4.1 Consensus Mechanisms: An Introduction

Consensus mechanisms allow a decentralized network to arrive at an agreement about the current network state [1]. In a centralized system or federal organization, all the decisions are taken by a single elected leader or a board of members, whereas in a decentralized network, a leader will not be available to take decision independently; instead, a group of systems/nodes are involved in the decision-making process. This process supports a decision, subject to the interest of all the people involved in the decision-making process, called a consensus. The mechanism used to achieve consensus in a distributed, decentralized network is defined as consensus mechanisms. These consensus mechanisms are the backbones of the heavily disruptive technology blockchain. In voting systems, the solution with the majority of votes wins; there is no weight for emotions or the welfare of the minority. In consensus systems, a decision is made for the benefit of the whole group scattered around the system, paving the way to create a more democratic and nondiscriminatory society. The famous implementation of blockchain is Bitcoin: a cryptocurrency implemented using the consensus mechanism. Behind any cryptocurrency in today's world, there exists a consensus mechanism. Consensus protocols also ensure mutual agreement [2] is reached in the cryptocurrency and there is no double spending.

4.2 Distributed Consensus Algorithms

Distributed consensus algorithms are the algorithms designed for reaching consensus in a distributed environment. The reached consensus should be a satisfactory solution supported by every individual in the network, even though it is not their personal favorite solution. These algorithms make sure the next block/value added to the system is the one and only version of truth. This way we can define consensus as a vibrant way of reaching a general agreement and commonality of faith within the group. Figure 4.1 shows an illustration of a consensus

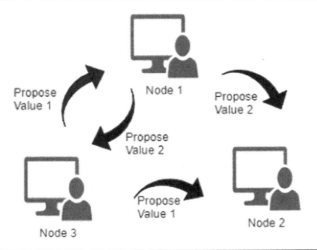

Figure 4.1 Consensus Model.

problem using three nodes, Node 1, Node 2, and Node 3. Node 1 proposes "value 2," Node 3 proposes "value 1" to the other nodes, and Node 2 keeps quiet. Consensus algorithms should be designed in a way to address this problem model and ultimately reach some value.

Distributed consensus algorithms exhibit the following properties to make the system work appropriately and prevent them from failures or glitches [3].

1. Collaboration – All the nodes in the system should work together with the interest of the whole group as the objective.
2. Cooperation – System entities should work as a group rather than an individual with personal interests.
3. Inclusive – Make sure there is a maximum number of participation from the group.
4. Participatory – Active participation by the group is required for being successful.
5. Agreement Seeking – Bring as much as agreement as possible from the individual nodes participating in the system.
6. Democratic – Each and every vote cast by the individuals should have an equal weight.

A consensus algorithm following the previously mentioned properties forms the primary root structure of the revolutionary technology

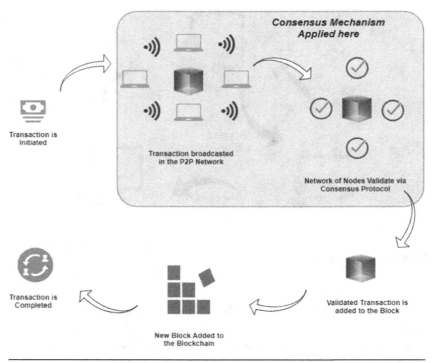

Figure 4.2 Application of Consensus in Blockchain.

blockchain. Consensus algorithms deployed in various blockchains makes them differ from each other. This functionality enables millions of nodes to exist in the same space, while they never exist mutually or hinder each other.

The processes highlighted in Figure 4.2 show the application of consensus algorithms in blockchain. Such consensus algorithms reaches consensus if the following conditions are satisified [4,5]:

1. Agreement – Each one of the nonfaulty nodes in the network should decide on the same output value.
2. Termination – Each and every nonfaulty node should ultimately decide on some output value. This is the termination condition.

There are a lot of consensus algorithms designed and implemented in real-world use cases, but each of those algorithms may vary in terminology, validity conditions (to achieve the final output value), and procedures on handling the decision-making process.

4.2.1 Nakamoto Consensus (Proof of Work)

A Nakamoto consensus can be defined as a probabilistic approach that is nondeterministic in nature. In this model every node need not agree on the same value; instead, they agree on the probability of the value being correct. This consensus mechanism is proved to have the following characteristics through its famous implementation Bitcoin:

1. Byzantine fault tolerance – There is no leader election in this process; instead, the decision is dependent on the nodes solving the computational puzzle faster and getting a chance to propose its value.
2. Incentive mechanism – When a node solves the puzzle and proposes a value agreed to by other nodes, an economic incentive is rewarded to the winner node.
3. Sybil resistance – Rather than using the conventional PKI authentication scheme or any other scheme, a proof of work (POW) mechanism is involved in the consensus process, making sure the process is Sybil resistant.
4. Gossip protocol – The peer-to-peer gossip protocol ensures messages are routed to all the nodes in the asynchronous network, assuming each node is connected to a subsection of nodes only.

4.2.1.1 Protocol Design   Nakamoto consensus is designed on the basis of the principle that all the nodes present in the Blockchain network run an identical protocol and manages their own copy of the decentralized ledger. This protocol depends on the fact that the majority of the nodes present in the network are honest or nonfaulty nodes.

Important rules applied in the design of the protocol [5,6] are mentioned next:

1. Message broadcasting rule – All the transactions, whether generated locally or received from other peer nodes within the network, should be broadcast to the identified peers in a timely manner without causing any delay. The same condition applies for broadcasting the blocks as well.

2. Validity – All the transactions and blocks received by each node should be validated before broadcasting. Once all the transactions in the blocks are validated, along with the block as a whole, it should be appended to the blockchain. Invalid transactions or blocks will be discarded in this process.

3. Longest-chain rule – In this consensus mechanism, any longest chain present in the network will be considered the valid chain. Any honest or nonfaulty node will build on top of the longest chain by appending the next valid block. The decision on where to append the next block will be reliant on the total amount of computation effort put on the longest chain.

4. Mining process – The POW is the backbone of Nakamoto consensus, taking care of a valid block generation process. Each node trying to propose a block should find a nonce (a number used once) to be inserted into the block header. The difficulty in finding the nonce will be adjusted periodically to certify the average block generation speed remains constant within the network.

Nakamoto consensus is apparently advantageous over the tradition consensus mechanism based on the following points:

1. Nakamoto consensus is Byzantine fault tolerant, though most of the traditional consensuses are not.

2. Any number of nodes can join or leave the network at any point of time, assuring open participation.

3. The nodes in the network need not know all the participants in the network; still they will have a finite set of known peers.

4. There is no communication overhead involved, unlike the traditional mechanisms.

5. A leader election process is not required in Nakamoto consensus.

4.2.1.2 Limitations

1. Nodes mining the next block try to use brute computing force. Hence, there is higher energy and computational power consumption for calculating the hash.

2. The average size of a block is limited to 1 MB, and the number

of transactions processed per block is quite less (approximately seven transactions per second). Other established networks like VISA and PayPal process much higher transactions within the same duration (~10,000 transactions per second in VISA).

4.3 Proposed Model: Proof of Virtue

The new model proposes to circumvent the higher energy and computational resource consumption in the famous POW consensus of Bitcoin. This is done by removing the tougher energy- and resource-intensive nonce identification for block hash generation. Bitcoin has proved safe from all the double-spending attacks using this puzzle calculation. What will happen if we remove this step from the processing? An alternative way is to introduce a new mechanism that is less resource intensive than public blockchain. Since this is a permissionless, public blockchain network, it can accommodate any number of participants joining the network.

The proposed model in Figure 4.3 follows similar steps as the regular Bitcoin processing, except the caveats in the hash calculation process mentioned here:

1. Each node in the system has an associated credit point (like a credit score in a fiat economy).
2. Any number of nodes can join the network or leave the network at will, which makes it a public blockchain like Bitcoin.
3. Any node that has a minimum threshold of credit points will be allowed for block generation. The initial network will generate a genesis block and n test blocks before any real transaction happens. This will test the reliability of the nodes participating in the network.
4. Let the minimum time required for generating a block be t. Then the time taken for the initial network to be set up will be

$$t_i = (n + 1)^* t$$

5. After the initial setup, each participating node that validated all the test blocks correctly will possess a credit of c_i. Let us consider the credit provided for validating a block correctly is c_1, and then initial credit will be

$$c_i = n^* c_1$$

6. The proposed model will set the threshold for participating in block generation as initial credit c_i.
7. While proposing the generated block, the node should pledge the accumulated credit points and incentives.
8. Block hash generation happens without calculating the nonce, which saves the computational and other energy resources.
9. All the nodes may participate in the validation of a new block generated.
10. Once the block is successfully validated, the generator of the block will get an incentive and rise in credit points
11. Each node successfully validating the generated block will also get a credit increase (although minimal).
12. If a block is not found to be valid, then the generator of the block will be penalized. The entire credit score is wiped off and incentives will be nullified.
13. Credit points and incentives will persist even if the user exits and enters the network as per his availability.
14. If one of the nodes or a few nodes in the system crash, they will be restored to the latest state by synchronizing with the other operating nodes. The recovered node will accept the longest chain from its peer nodes and continues to contribute to the network.
15. Participating peer nodes will instantly broadcast any new blocks they know about in the system. Hence if there is any latency, disorder, or loss of messages in the network, the network will be out of sync for some time; however, the synchronization process between each node balances it eventually, similar to the recovery mechanism used in Bitcoin blockchain.

4.3.1 New User Joining the Network

Any new user who joins the network will start with zero credits. As soon as they join the network, the user will not be fully functional. He can validate the generated blocks and increase his credit points; however, he may not be able to generate new blocks. This will ensure the network is Sybil resistant. The credit points will be added to the user only when the

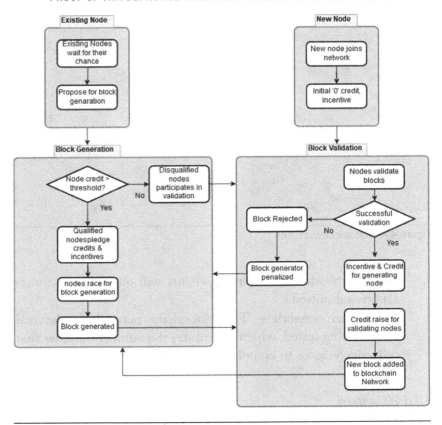

Figure 4.3 Flow Diagram: Proof of Virtue.

block he has validated is successfully added to the network. Once the new user gets the minimum required credit, he will be allowed to participate in block generation, thus becoming fully functional.

4.3.2 Performance Requirements

1. A test network, as shown in Figure 4.4, will have a number of clients to inject the workload and make interpretations based on the observations made. Clients are the platforms/entities that directly interact with the blockchain network rather than the application built on top of it.
2. Clients – Load-generating clients will submit new transactions

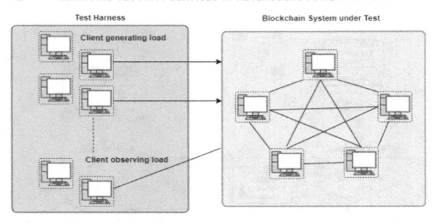

Figure 4.4 Performance Evaluation.

to the network, and observing clients will only observe transactions submitted.
3. Blockchain network – The blockchain network is the real system being tested, which constitutes the number of nodes that collectively agree to complete transactions.

4.3.3 Advantages

1. Energy and other resource waste is brought down due to the removal of nonce (puzzle) generation in the hash generation process.
2. Mining power does not play any role in block generation, which prevents 51% of attacks.
3. A new user has to wait for a certain period until he gets the required credit score for participating in the block generation process, which will make the network Sybil resistant.
4. Since there is no restriction on the minimum time taken for block generation, the transaction speed will be increased, making the system more scalable.
5. The consensus mechanism applied for the block verification and validation makes the system Byzantine fault tolerant.

4.3.4 Limitations

1. The security of the network will be measured based on the total number of participating nodes in the network. If there are only few nodes participating in the network, there is a high possibility for centralization of power.
2. Nodes have to validate test blocks for initial credits during the primary setup of the network.

4.4 Conclusion and Future Work

Consensus algorithms are used for the systems in a distributed environment to reach a collective agreement. There cannot be any distributed or decentralized system without a consensus mechanism implemented to reach an agreement. The nodes within a network may not trust each other, but they have to comply with the consensus algorithms to decide on a common goal. Blockchain may build blocks from innumerable transactions, forming a database, but they would not be decentralized in nature without the consensus algorithms. The famous POW consensus mechanism is also not free from criticism of its computational and resource-intensive process. Our new mechanism, proof of virtue, will overcome these drawbacks at the same time and is resistant to 51% of Sybil attacks and any kind of malfunctioning. Though the mechanism has been carefully devised, intensive testing needs to be done – this will be a scope for future work.

References

1. Hong Guo, Hongqiang Zheng, Kai Xu, Xiangrui Kong, Jing Liu, Fang Liu, and Keke Gai, "An Improved Consensus Mechanism for Blockchain," Springer Nature Switzerland, (2018), https://doi.org/10.1007/978-3-030-05764-0_14.
2. Deepak Puthal, Nisha Malik, Saraju P. Mohanty, Elias Kougianos, and Gautam Das, "Everything You Wanted to Know About the Blockchain," IEEE Consumer Electronics magazine, (2018), DOI: 10.1109/MCE.2018.2816299.
3. https://101blockchains.com/consensus-algorithms-blockchain/, Online, Accessed on 01/11/2019.
4. John Turek, and Dennis Shasha, "The Many Faces of Consensus in Distributed Systems," IEEE Computer, 1992.
5. V. Gramoli, "From blockchain consensus back to Byzantine consensus," Future Generation Computer Systems, (2017), http://dx.doi.org/10.1016/j.future.2017.09.023.
6. S. Nakamoto, "Bitcoin: A peer-to-peer electronic cash system," 2008.

5

PASSWORD AUTHENTICATION USING KEYSTROKE BIOMETRIC

SHUBHAM SOOD AND M. VANITHA

School of Information Technology and EngineeringVellore Institute of Technology, Vellore-632014, Tamil Nadu, India

Contents

5.1 Introduction

Authentication is the process of confirming whether the user is the one it pretends to be. It is utilized as a method for distinguishing substantial or legitimate clients from the impostors. Password-based confirmation is the most broadly utilized client validation component. This strategy utilizes a brief for a username and password that is one of a kind to a specific client. A password must be exclusive, long, complex, and strong. A person must use different passwords for different applications. Using a comparable password for various applications makes it continuously feeble to attacks. A strong password involves any blend of lowercase letters, uppercase letters, numerals, unique characters, and images that have a length of eight characters or more. Keeping passwords simple makes them subject to attacks. Knowing someone's user ID and password makes it very easy for an intruder to get into the system. Getting a person's password is not difficult in this age of technology where everything is digital.

Therefore, there needs to be some way to sustain authentication even if someone knows gets to know your password.

The proposed work gives a solution for this loophole in the password authentication system. It uses the typing behavior of a person to recognize the user. Studies have shown that each person has a certain pattern while he is typing; therefore, it can be used to distinguish between users. Keystroke elements allude to the computerized technique for recognizing or affirming the personality of an individual dependent on the way and the rhythm of composing on a keyboard. Keystroke elements is a behavioral biometric; this implies the biometric factor is "something you do".

The crude estimations utilized for keystroke elements are abiding time and flight time.

1. **Dwell time**: the time duration that a key is pressed
2. **Flight time**: the time in the middle of discharging a key and pressing the following key

The rhythm with which a few groupings of characters are composed can be very individual dependent. The focal point of this exploration is to examine the client authentication to forestall ill-conceived client access by using secret phrase keystroke elements as multifaceted verification. This examination is finished by utilizing dynamic time traveling for similitude estimation; the validation framework is tried utilizing the dataset before introduced to the client for framework convenience scale poll. To improve the performance of the authentication system, several techniques have been incorporated with the biometric authentication system to check the pattern of the user for authentication with the help of the KNN algorithm, which will allow you to enter into the cluster zone, which is saved by the user at the time of registration, where the Euclidean distance formula will help you to check the saved cluster and will allow you to access the page or will deny the access. Users have accepted keystroke dynamics since it is cheap, as only a keyboard is required for authenticating the user before accessing an application. The dynamic framework keeps on observing the 'client's keystroke through the course of the cooperation even though passing the sign-in meeting effectively. It implies that the composing example of an individual is continually investigated progressively for guaranteeing the personality of the client during the full length of the meeting

5.2 Related Works

Faisal Alshanketi et al. [1] purposed the irregular timberlands calculation to improve the exactness execution of keystroke dynamic biometric verification. We additionally proposed a novel calculation for dealing with composing botches. Re-enactments results on the openly accessible what's more, our gathered informational indexes demonstrate that the proposed methodology yields significantly better execution results. Besides utilizing finger weight and territory alongside the planning highlights fundamentally improves the exhibition of the proposed plan. Notwithstanding the biometric factor, utilizing fixed secret phrase strings can be helpless against replay assaults. A modern key lumberjack can be used to sniff the secret phrase with keystroke elements, which would then be able to be reused to get entrance to the secured framework. One way to alleviate such risk is to extricate the keystroke elements from a one-time secret word (OTP). This methodology still presents huge difficulties in the wording of precision.

Farida Jaha et al. [2] have proposed a solid secret word strategy that can give verification security for the client. Nevertheless, if another individual can uncover the secret word, no secret word strategy can avert an unapproved client from getting entrance. With the utilization of dynamic keystrokes, the impostor assault is pointless because dynamic composing is a novel component to each individual. In light of numerous quests, we reason those keystroke elements can be a dependable security instrument for verification. Dynamic composing is a system that permits the protected utilization of bring your own device (BYOD) in organizations. It doesn't require extra speculation. Along these lines, organizations are receiving the rewards of BYOD without being casualties of information leakage. For those and different reasons we presented a pseudo code to execute keystroke elements utilizing stay time capacities as well as weight time capacities. To think about the information entered utilizing the console and storing biometric information, we picked the Euclidean separation, which will be contrasted and limits decided by the framework director to acknowledge or dismiss the client. Building up an application that executes the dynamic keystroke will be an extraordinary advantage to all clients and especially organizations; this progression will be the subject of future research.

Purvashi Baynath et al. [3] proposed an innovation that is commonly utilized for distinguishing proof and access control, or for recognizing. The fundamental reason for biometric validation is that everybody is unmistakable—what's more, an individual can be distinguished by their central physical or conduct characteristics. A biometric framework alongside its joining with the secret word has given another way to further improve security. Keystroke elements have been acknowledged by clients, as it is effectively deployable at the client's end. Many works have been investigated in the field of keystroke dynamics, and anyway in other biometric applications the neural system that emulates the client example is an exceptionally encouraging procedure to be utilized. By dissecting the current biometrics, it very well may be expressed that the uses of the tumultuous neural system alongside the biometric highlights give superior security than other methods. The disordered neural system approach for learning biometric examples is an integral asset to enhance the acknowledgment pace of the biometric system. Accordingly, this method has been connected to two databases to be specific to our inbuilt database and one online database where the element measurement decrease method has been tried. From the test, it tends to be seen that the riotous neural system gives a superior acknowledgment rate.

Carlo Ferrari et al. [4] displayed an adaptive continuous biometric validation system, which uses keystroke elements to check the asserted character of a client while he or she is composing on a figuring framework (and presumably getting to a few administrations that must be verified). The utilization of a conduct biometric parameter spares computational assets and vitality and it doesn't require extra equipment. All together to bring down the affectability of the frameworks to anticipated changes in the manner a client is composing, because of fatigue, tiredness, or disposition, each certified client model is ceaselessly recomputed while information from composing is recorded. Simultaneously, to the models of the other selected clients are recomputed previously coordinating, bringing about a superior framework. In a future work, adaptability issues ought to be tended to as well as the acquaintance of mouse elements with getting a stronger framework. A cautious upgrade of the component vector and the concurrent utilization of two unique measurements in the model correlation for choice could likewise improve the simplicity, the speed, and the exactness of the testing strategy. Finally, the proposed framework ought to be approved in some remarkably genuine applications like webmail, online test, and checking of a basic site.

Santanu Chatterjee et al. [5] purposed another Chebyshev riotous guide-based lightweight multiserver confirmation plot. We have utilized the arbitrary prophet model and the BAN rationale for formal security examination and reproduced our plan utilizing the broadly acknowledged AVISPA device for the formal security check. The outcomes demonstrate that our plan is secure from surely understood potential assaults required in a multiserver condition. Also, our plan satisfies known usefulness highlights pertinent to a multiserver condition. Our plan does not require association of the RC during the login and validation and key-foundation stage. As an outcome, our plan is effective and progressively reasonable for pragmatic applications, particularly for portable and battery-controlled gadgets when contrasted with other existing plans.

Puja Smriti et al. [6] purposed keystroke elements are the social biometric strategy that is utilized for confirmation or checking the character of the client dependent on the composing cadence of the person. In this chapter, we proposed a novel strategy to correspond to the keystroke information of a personal computer with that of the workstation. The results acquired are exceptionally energizing. In the future, the comparative approach could be tried on different sorts of consoles. More highlights can be included to improve the exactness. Further, the methodology might be tried for cell phones too.

Michael J. Coakley et al. [7] has come up with the primary objective of this examination was to break down the confirmation execution of the different sorts of text entry biometric data that can be removed from the present cell phones. The conventional timing keypress/key-discharge has obtained 20% EER compared to the existing mechanical consoles. Then again, the amazing outcomes accomplished by the touchscreen highlights (4.0% EER) and the spinner just included (4.3% EER) seem to offer a convincing methodology towards client confirmation on cell phones. Two diverse approval techniques (RRS and LOOCV) were looked at in the investigation and, true to form, the LOOCV strategy gave preferred outcomes over RRS, yet to the detriment of more prominent calculation time. Of the two separation measurements analyzed, the Manhattan separation outflanked the Euclidean separation reliably all through the majority of the trials, notwithstanding the list of capabilities utilized. It is intriguing to see that the customary planning key-press/key-discharge, including those accessible on mechanical consoles, give flimsier execution results when compared to touchscreens. In expansion to the structure factor, the vibe of individual keys on mechanical consoles cultivates progressively steady and repeatable keystroke elements contrasted with the level, to some degree dangerous feel of the virtual consoles on touchscreens. This is a region justifying further examination.

Md Liakat Ali et al. [8] have come up with numerous specialists who have not focused on the computational cost of preparing and testing a KD framework. A vigorous KD framework ought to be responsive, particularly if the application requires a continuous connection. A few works have been directed on free or long content info, yet they have utilized just English as the essential language of correspondence. An examination of the convertibility to different dialects is justified. Future research ought to likewise put more prominent accentuation on cell phones with an immense range of sensors. Numerous gadgets support multicontact screens, weight touchy boards, accelerometers, and other features, all of which could be consolidated into a KD framework.

Information gathering in many investigations was performed over a generally brief timeframe. The composing conduct of people may change because of age, well-being, or energy state. Recently have we seen studies about that endeavor to identify the psychological burden from composing conduct and how client impediments influence KD framework execution. At last, creating benchmark datasets for the KD validation will be promising future research. KD datasets ought to consider factors, for example, input gadget, input type, and input length, so that KD frameworks can be assessed because of these criteria. Future work ought to likewise endeavor to offer a clarification on why a specific strategy accomplishes better execution. Advancement of an institutionalized convention for KD frameworks may help make various works tantamount. KD research is still in the underlying stage, and an exceptionally constrained number of studies have been led so far contrasted with other biometric frameworks. Although it has favorable circumstances such as minimal effort, straightforwardness, noninvasive for the client, and nonstop verification, it has low exactness contrasted with other biometric frameworks.

Maria Habib Ja'far Alqatawna [9] discusses a study on the current biometric procedures. Biometrics could be physical (fingerprint, iris, palm, face acknowledgment) and behavioral (keystroke elements, voice, and stride). Besides, it talks about their points of interest, hindrances, and the assessment measurements utilized in biometric execution measures. Likewise, it diagrams on-going biometric multimodal plans (physiological, social, and half breed), including their shortcomings and impediments. In conclusion, it proposes another combination confirmation plan of vein and keystroke elements.

Md. Asraful Haque [10] discusses a study on the examination that our strategy is very straightforward since it depends on factual methodology and gives intriguing outcomes with over 93% precision. We accept that the approach will effectively overcome numerous assaults, which regular secret key security components neglect to vanquish. In any case, there are still some potential issues in our plan which should be referenced. To start with, there is no numerical rationale behind choosing the edge. It has been chosen distinctly via cautious tuning of the outcomes. Second, we have contemplated the qualities of keystroke elements for a customary PC console gadget. Along these lines, composing speed in the virtual console may differ for a similar client. Third, the enrollment procedure is time consuming and exhausting for the clients. Our analysis does not manage these circumstances. In any case, there are numerous degrees in the proposed frameworks which can be considered for further enhancements. One of the methods for improving the framework's execution is to refresh the client composing profile with time. Another approach to improve the outcome is to locate the sensible limit by utilizing some sort of scientific examination. The blunder rate can be diminished if we enable the clients to utilize the delete key for the amendment of the secret word. Any future change should diminish the false-positive and false-negative mistakes. The utilization of cell phones, tablets, and other touchscreen gadgets are picking up notoriety with an amazing pace lately.

Sung-Shiou et al. [11] discusses a study on current PC or versatile interchanges framework that depends significantly on utilizing the username/secret key verification strategy to ensure the framework information. Eventually, the old-style verification strategy experiences numerous security defects and convenience constraints. Today an entrancing biometrics confirmation instrument, elements keystroke, is one of the celebrated biometric advances. This paper expands the dynamic keystroke idea and proposes a weight-based dynamic keystroke approach as greater security and useable unique keystroke confirmation elective. Catching and breaking down extra client key code (key mood and key weight) and timestamp during the enlistment stage progressively upgrades the fruitful probability of the confirmation procedure and security more. Besides, the equipment and the product subsystem model usage additionally demonstrates the achievability and ease of use of the proposed validation plot in this writing

Yekta Said Can et al. [12] proposed utilizing keystroke elements D variable Gaussian, KNN, and choice tree for the acknowledgment framework calculations were tried on the CMU keypress database. CMU keystroke was utilized as the database. The best characterization precision rate among the calculations k was the closest neighbor calculation. At the point when k is 8 victories were gotten. KNN more than article utilizing the equivalent dataset gave victories. Moreover, the DD time, flight, and keypress provided better characterization when utilized, notwithstanding a period where the KNN calculation provided better outcomes.

Purvashi Baynath et al. [13] dissected the current biometrics, and it very well may be plainly said that the use of a neural system alongside the biometric highlights gives superior security than other procedures. In this paper, the classifier neural system joined with keystroke elements accomplishes a superior security framework. The neural system can deal with a huge measure of the dataset, and it can likewise verifiably distinguish complex, nonstraight connections among ward and nonsubordinate factors. The neural system is currently picking up consideration in the advancement of keystroke elements. Since the last have accomplished noteworthy acknowledgment rate in other biometric frameworks, it is inspiring for specialists to investigate the plausibility of applying this system on keystroke elements.

Chandralekha Jadhav et al. [14] proposed model that gives a development-level security to basic frameworks where security is one of the significant concerns. The model does not require any additional equipment like other physiological biometric frameworks do and subsequently, the general expense is extensively insignificant. We utilized five parameters for our validation model utilizing which a framework that gives a FAR and FRR of 1% and 4% separately. Since FAR and FRR both portray the wrong acknowledgments, these qualities should be insignificant. Our model accomplishes the ideal and adequate scope of these qualities. It is a difficult task to remove the false acceptance rate and false rejection rate. In this way, taking out these parameters altogether would be one significant assignment that necessities to be dealt with conveniently in the up and coming variants of this task. Varieties inexactness can be brought about by the varieties in composing musicality that could be brought about by other factors, for example, damage, weariness, tranquilize impact, or diversion. The framework must be large enough to decrease such imperfections. Another restriction is that because of customization towards a secret phrase, developing composing capability, adjustment to include gadgets, and other natural factors, the composing example is exposed to change. We have to deal with these adjustments in a clever way. Likewise, more spotlights on making this framework dynamic are anticipated.

Made Indra Wira Pramana et al. [15] proposed the technique for keystroke elements validation might be usable, all things considered, for client SUS score of the framework which is better than expected to arrive at 70; notwithstanding, there are still more to create before the technique is prepared to be connected. The displayed technique results in FAR of 39.9% and FRR of 3.3%—this outcome needs greater improvement. The technique results in EER of 17.6%, a lot higher than the outcome from the dataset maker. A high EER might be brought about by the client, not used to the characterized fixed content on the dataset age. While clients point out that the strategy is usable, some improvement is expected to further expand the execution of the technique to appropriately recognize an ill-conceived client from a genuine client.

Jiaju Huang et al. [16] came up with the KDE calculation that indicates comparative execution on the Bison, Clarkson, and Torino datasets. Generally, KDE makes the most reliable, stable execution. Not only does it have the most comparative presentation on different datasets, its exhibition on our unconstrained dataset (Clarkson II) debases the least. The Genetti and Picardi calculation performs more regrettably on the Buffalo dataset, yet comparative on the other two. The SVM calculation has a comparative execution on the Buffalo dataset and Clarkson I, yet much more regrettable on Torino, since it does not have the key discharge time the calculation requires. We may presume that since each of the three datasets are gathered in comparable settings, they have comparable execution. The contrasts among English and Italian appear to have no role in the process. Then again, our very own new, unconstrained dataset (Clarkson II) is made out of composing during a member's ordinary figuring conduct and incorporates keystrokes from an assortment of exercises, just as uproarious keystrokes from exercises, for example, gaming. It makes the most noticeably terrible execution for every one of the three calculations; however, it is bound to mirror the truth of genuine keystroke elements. The quantity of highlights is basic for keystroke elements validation has demonstrated that the more digraphs utilized, the better the exhibition. However, the number of highlights that it uses is still far not exactly from those utilized by the KDE and Gunetti and Picardi's calculations. Along these lines, much more terrible execution is found for this calculation. In particular, since there is no key discharge time in the Torino dataset, just one of the three required highlights is utilized. As a result, we see a sharp decrease in its validation execution.

Chaitanya Dwivedi [17] shows a study on dependent on keystroke elements, in contrast to other grouping issues, described by explicit subtleties that must be remembered. Such subtleties call for extraordinary techniques for pre-preparing and expansion. It tends to be seen that the feasibility of keystroke-based framework confirmation is subject to satisfactory classifier choice, information preparation, and classifier tuning. The paper efficiently manages all these issues.

Further, it proposes a novel half-breed classifier to bargain with appropriate issues like low precision and high EER present in contemporary methodologies for keystroke elements-based client verification. Future work may incorporate performing keystroke elements on a free message. Parameters, for example, mouse developments, and GUI cooperation, and so on, might be utilized as extra highlights to improve classifier execution.

Md Liakat Ali et al. [18] discuss a study on generative and discriminative models that have different preferences and impediments in biometric applications. Generative models can deal with absent or novel information. Discriminative models are normally exceptionally quick at ordering new information and would have preferable prescient execution over the generative models. While trying to look for preferences from both generative and discriminative models, this investigation proposes a crossbreed POHMM/SVM model. The proposed model has accomplished a lower equivalent mistake rate in client confirmation contrasted and other distributed work maintaining the benchmark assessment methodology for static verification. The future work will be to apply the proposed crossbreed model with a free message-based dataset for client-recognizable proof and check the reason. The proposed half and half POHMM/SVM model is composed of a generative model POHMM and a discriminative model SVM. POHMM fills in as a highlights extractor and SVM fills in as a classifier in the proposed model. This gives more noteworthy solidarity to the proposed crossbreed model to accomplish predominant check results with the short-fixed content based dataset. As the POHMM/SVM employments discriminative model SVM for arrangement, the mixture POHMM/SVM model additionally anticipated accomplishing better execution in the free message dataset for persistent validation. For the reason that the exhibition accomplished for POHMM/SVM in this examination is utilizing just a solitary solid word (secret key) and inconsistent verification, keystroke elements can, without much of a stretch, catch a large dataset from every client to accomplish higher validation execution.

Jigyasa Handa et al. [19] proposed that keystroke examination and mouse elements play an imperative job in a social biometrics study. Information picked up from all the above data moves one to know more about the future utilization of these two strategies in security and different fields of the digital world. The mouse elements can be further institutionalized based on the mouse pointer speed. Keystroke examination provides information about composing styles of a client, and it can be utilized as one-of-a-kind personality of a person.

Debasis Giri et al. [20] purposed a proficient common verification convention that has been displayed to encode documents in a Universal Serial Bus (USB) Mass Storage Device (MSD) empowering secure and usable "USB memory sticks". This paper has contributed a novel idea to the present best in class in biometric security calculations by safeguarding against security assaults and improving gadget convenience crosswise over various sessions. Besides, the paper has officially demonstrated that the proposed convention can withstand important security shortcomings. An execution correlation has likewise been made with the writing to affirm that the proposed plan accomplishes an altogether lower calculation cost and correspondence cost than other related plans. The general effectiveness exhibits that USB-based MSDs with biometric security sensors can be executed to give critical security and ease of use for the customer.

V. Chandrasekar [21] has come up with an attempt to give a thorough overview of research on keystroke elements. The procedures were ordered dependent on the highlights, including extraction techniques utilized, and their exhibition has been examined. It has been seen that the vast majority of the work utilized keystroke span, inactivity, and digraph as highlights, and the joined utilization of these highlights prompts low FAR. Keystroke biometrics has a favorable position over a large portion of the other biometric verification plans, in particular, client acknowledgment. Since clients are as of now acclimated with verifying themselves through username and passwords, most proposed keystroke biometric strategies are straightforward. Keystroke biometrics has additionally demonstrated extraordinary potential, as the highlights can be gathered without the requirement for any exceptional equipment.

Jiyun Wu et al. [22] proposed a personality confirmation framework dependent on keystroke practices that have considered the adjustments in clients' motion. This framework gathers five highlights (i.e. keystroke speeding up, weight, size, time, and gadget direction) in a certain way while a client is opening the cell phone. Likewise, it takes a progression of measures to improve the framework's precision, for example, subfeature determination, information standardized pre-processing, and parameter advancement for SVM. What's more, it is the first endeavor to consider the progressions in many signals in character validation. We gave our work a trial study, and our investigations demonstrate that the framework's EER of considering the progressions of motion is 1.2514% lower than the instance of not considering. Likewise, we utilize an assortment of examination errands to survey the effect of different factors on the cell phone confirmation framework. Even though the framework has a decent presentation in its precision, there is as yet far to go. Right off the bat, this sort of framework just applies to open the touch screen, and it will lose a significant barrier if a cell phone is open. In this way, it is huge to think about the constant personality confirmation for cell phones, that is, whatever status the cell phone is, the character verification framework will keep running out of sight quietly and recognize the client consistently, and it won't expend an excess of battery control; furthermore, not just the progressions of the signal will cause a few contrasts of validation results—additionally a client's condition of movement will make the information unique. For instance, the keystroke activity is variable or even has a major distinction when the client is stopped and strolling or sitting and lying. Thus, including increasingly ecological contemplations or catching some new social highlights which are not influenced by them requires further request; at long last, there are some different executions of our personality confirmation framework, including how to acquire information tests helpfully for the preparation stage and how to shield the framework from being effectively wrecked by the intrusion.

Asma Salem et al. [23] proposed an exploration study that led to a broad investigation of the conduct verification frameworks dependent on KSD. We investigated the field from alternative points of view. Primary highlights were extricated and the approaches to be utilized are featured. Numerous methodologies were done to structure and actualize a confirmation frameworks dependent on KSD in this examination, and a near investigation with contending works is additionally given. KSD gives a substantial trademark a satisfactory level in execution measures as a second-factor validation implies. This social-based framework is the most affordable second-factor verification strategy because no extra equipment is required or added to the execution. Timing and non-timing blend in the investigation of highlights can improve the security level of KSD confirmation frameworks. Besides, the accompanying headings can be embraced to accomplish the smallest blunder rates in the confirmation. There is a need to discover great strategies for highlights gathering and extractions. The benchmarking needs in this field are the primary test for doing a right similar investigation.

Han Honggui et al. [24] finds that issue identification is one of the center research zones in the field of WWTP. A shortcoming recognition framework, fusing the anticipating plant and issue finding technique is proposed and applied to a WWTP as a contextual analysis. In the anticipating plant, a smart approach, FNN, is created to improve the exactness of the SVI expectations. What's more, the intermingling of the proposed FNN approach has been explicitly structured as a primary concern. The execution of the versatile foreseeing plant dependent on FNN affirms that this clever methodology can upgrade the limit of the SVI anticipating plant as for the qualities of WWTP. The examination results show that the versatile foreseeing plant can yield more precise SVI expectations than different strategies. Then, a flaw finding technique, because of the residuals of the forecasts and the SVI sensor, is created to uncover the issues on the web. Exploratory outcomes demonstrate that the proposed deficiency location framework is of identifying the exact issues of the SVI sensor, which is basic to keep the sheltered and conservative activity of WWTP.

Chao Shen et al. [25] proposed expanding security familiarity with the secret key from people in general and little consideration on the qualities of genuine passwords, it is consequently normal to comprehend the present state of qualities of genuine passwords and to investigate how secret word attributes change after some time and how the prior secret key practice is comprehended in the current setting. Right now, we endeavor to show an inside and out and thorough comprehension of client practice in genuine passwords, and to see whether the past perceptions can be affirmed or switched, in light of huge scale estimations as opposed to narrative information or client overviews. In particular, we measure secret word attributes on more than 6 million passwords, as far as secret word length, secret phrase piece, and secret phrase selection. We then make educated examinations of the discoveries between our examination and recently revealed outcomes. Our general discoveries include: (1) normal secret phrase length is at any rate 12% longer than past results, and 75% of our passwords have the length somewhere in the range of 8 and 10 characters; (2) there is a huge increment of utilizing just numbers as passwords, and simple to-arrive at images are consistently the primary decision when clients included images into passwords; (3) there watches a noteworthy increment (about 40%) of utilizing combo-significant information like passwords, and a striking extent of utilizing the most widely recognized passwords or login names as passwords. Our examination additionally incorporates gathering measurements about the utilization of images, letter-case, and significant subtleties, which introduces an efficient investigation of secret key utilization. The relative results demonstrate that the secret word qualities and secret key practice on this monstrous secret word informational index are to some degree conflicting with those from recounted information and client overviews and display a considerable change after some time somehow or another. Further research requirements to expand upon this comprehension for picking up knowledge into how secret phrase security can be improved.

Nimbhorkar [26] has come up with practically, an underlying one-time login check is insufficient to address the hazard that is associated with post signed in session. In this way this paper endeavors to give such an exhaustive study of research on the basic structure squares required to assemble a persistent biometric validation framework. The absolute first test is the decision of biometric. The test of inaccessibility of perception of at least one modality at a specific time is tended to in the segment on a combination of modalities. In addition, different existing strategies are utilized for constant verification utilizing multi-modular biometrics. Constant verification is a rising method that lessens the mistake rates, and to improve the precision and speed of the frameworks.

A Buchoux et al. [27] proposed keystroke investigation could be implementable on a portable handset actually and that clients would receive such a methodology. The measurable classifiers showed low handling prerequisites that can be utilized on a genuine gadget, with convenient reactions in both the layout age and check of tests. Regardless, the outcomes have indicated the significance of the sort of info utilized; with 4-digit PIN-based methodologies being excessively short by and by to utilize.

Arwa Alsultan et al. [28] come up with free-content keystroke elements is a non-meddlesome technique since it just uses the conduct information that clients pass on during standard composing errands. Notwithstanding that, it is moderately reasonable; the main required equipment is the console. Anyway, the most significant advantage that free-text keystroke frameworks give is that the composing designs can, in any case, be utilized for confirming clients much after the validation stage has passed. What's sans more content validation gives an important harmony between security and convenience which is exceptionally attractive in the organization's world? One worry about free-content keystrokes is that it tends to be instable as it may be affected by the client state or by ecological conditions. To be sure a few levels of insecurity may happen with no self-evident cause. Thusly, free-content validation is most likely best utilized as a piece of a multifaceted validation conspire that gives a more elevated level of security. For the most part, keystroke elements work all the more precisely for fixed-content contrasted and free-content. Consequently, it may be a decent practice for nothing content tests to think about the genuine words that the client is composing, notwithstanding the key hold time the diagram's length and idleness times. Additionally, deciding the best technique to follow to accomplish the best confirmation exactness isn't a direct undertaking. Because of the variety of conditions that may be influencing the examination members, condition, or on the other hand strategy, the examination between at least two strategies isn't constantly exact. Subsequently, an institutionalization component must be set up to guarantee that variables influencing execution are in understanding taking all things together with the investigations and thus can be appropriately thought about

Nandini Chourasia [29] proposed that client can get to the account. This application can be utilized in an android telephone or Smartphone through which we can get to the web and can perform the exchange. The approved client can without much of a stretch access their record and perform an exchange. The keystroke dynamic is supplanting the information-based and token-based confirmation framework. Anyway, the keystroke dynamic is more dependable, having minimal effort for usage, is straightforward, and the client doesn't perceive the foundation keystroke elements are being performed. The client who isn't of a specialized foundation can effectively get to because it doesn't require any specialized information.

Nader Abdel Karim et al. [30] proposed that client validation strategies can be information-based, ownership-based, or biometric based. Biometric-based confirmation is considered the most precise and well-known strategy in online tests to validate the client. Pantomime sway validity and is the fundamental risk that faces online test situations. It very well may be arranged into two kinds. A few business items use verification strategies to ensure online tests, for example, Secureexam, delegate, ProtorCam, Webassessor, and BIoSig_ID.

Clayton Epp et al. [31] proposed the capacity to perceive feelings is a significant piece of building savvy PCs. Frameworks that could remove the enthusiastic parts of a circumstance would have a rich setting from which to settle on fitting choices about step by step instructions to connect with the client or adjust their framework reaction. There are two fundamental issues with current methodologies for distinguishing feelings that point of confinement their pertinence: they can be intrusive and may require costly gear. We displayed an answer that decides client feeling by investigating the cadence of clients' composing designs on a standard console. To assemble inwardly marked information, we directed a field study where members' keystrokes were gathered and their states were recorded using self-report utilizing an encounter examining approach. From this information, we removed keystroke inclusions and diminished our highlight set utilizing a connection-based component subset property choice. We made classifiers for 15 states.

Romain Giot et al. [32] proposed another openly accessible dataset for keystroke elements. This dataset is made out of a few clients who have an alternate login and secret key. We think it is the most reasonable keystroke elements dataset which is freely accessible. We have factually confirmed that: (an) exhibiting EER figured with an individual limit, gives better outcome than registering the EER with a worldwide limit (which clarifies why a ton of keystroke elements contemplates utilizing this technique), (b) utilizing logins gives preferred execution over utilizing passwords, (c) utilizing all highlights during the combination improves the presentation, (d) the size and the entropy of the secret phrase affect the presentation. Keystroke elements is an intriguing methodology; nevertheless, it requires severe conditions during obtaining to stay away from the catch of various examples. This may infer an education of the client. As its execution diminishes a great deal with time, it is important to follow the time fluctuation into account which will be the following work on this dataset.

Kevin Casey [33] came up with a work indicating that keystroke measurements can add to increasingly precise pass-bomb classifiers; significantly, the element giving the best expectation exactness was that of program multifaceted nature. This component was acquired utilizing a system sketched out by Jbara and Feitelson (2014) where the length of the packed code was utilized as an intermediary for the multifaceted nature of the code understudies compose. Regardless, this is simply a guess for the program multifaceted nature, so future work in improving this element can yield significant advantages. While numerous different measurements could be added to the classifier, keystroke digraphs are especially fascinating. In particular, they are generally steady. Type-E digraph latencies don't shift massively from the time they are first precisely estimated. Conversely with different measurements, for example, the unpredictability of projects that understudies compose (which normally increments after some time as understudies learn), it is a perfect early-pointer. Not exclusively is a decent early pointer, digraph latencies likewise contribute something other than what's expected than other measurements that reflect exertion used by the understudy, for example, time spent on the stage or projects incorporated. Digraph latencies measure something inherent in the understudy capacities and, given the circumstances, are a significant subordinate to these understudy exertion related measurements.

Brajesh Singh et al. [34] have determined that an insider's assault is still the most serious issue to date. The proposed framework shows better outcomes in defeating such insider dangers. Likewise, the proposed framework doesn't require extra equipment for usage.

·Pin Shen The et al. [35] proposed the greater part of the keystroke elements inquire about works from the most recent three decades have been abridged and broke down in this paper. It is in no way, shape, or form to be a depleted file of all examination works in the keystroke elements space; however, it was gathered with the asset accessible and to the best of our insight at the purpose of writing. The point of this audit paper is to give a reference to specialists to additionally look into others' work to recognize promising examination bearing for further study. We accept that this will likewise fundamentally lower the passage hindrance particularly for amateur specialists who are keen on keystroke elements.

S.J. Shepherd [36] has come up with a show persistent validation programming system utilizing composing rhythm: has been created for the IBM PC. The framework is simple, easy, and gives precise measurements of keystroke term and interim. Starting investigations show that this information is prepared to do recognizing and distinguishing people. The product is stand-alone modules that can be consolidated effectively into ignore advanced security frameworks. The source code is uninhibitedly accessible to the individuals who wish to explore further.

Laura K. Allen et al. [37] presented an examination using various segments identified with the composing procedure to examine the adequacy of composing preparing frameworks to educate stealth evaluations regarding understudies' full of feeling states. Our inevitable objective is to utilize these stealth evaluations to improve our understudy models in the W-Pal framework, which will permit us to give understudies progressively customized criticism and guidance. All the more extensively, the present examination proposes that person contrasts, content lists, and internet composing measures, (for example, keystroke investigations) can be utilized as a stage towards progressively versatile instructive advancements for composing. Even though this is just a first step, and various examinations stay to be led, this investigation gives a solid starting establishment since it shows the possibility of such measures for demonstrating influence.

Terence Sim et al. [38] took a measurable example acknowledgment point of view, and explored the discriminability of digraphs, trigraphs, and so on. With regards to free-content keystroke elements. We indicated that conventional, non-word-explicit n-charts are not discriminative. This certifies the discoveries of different scientists. We indicated that, rather, word-explicit n-diagrams toll much better. We likewise indicated that for certain Sequences, its unique circumstance affects its timings. This drove us to plan a classifier that utilizations entire words for highlights. Our classifier accomplished an exhibition practically identical to the forefront.

Eesa Al Solami et al. [39] proposed the existing consistent biometric confirmation conspires and depicted example ceaseless verification situations. We distinguished the basic qualities and properties from the nonexclusive model of CBAS. To date, there is no CBAS conveyed in true applications, most likely since the current frameworks need reasonableness. We watched that the fundamental confinements are identified with the preparation information which forestalls CBAS to be material in reality applications. The issues are the prerequisite of the preparation information to be accessible ahead of time, too many preparing information tests required, the changeability of the conduct biometric between the preparation and testing stage if there should arise an occurrence of the correlation time, and the fluctuation of the conduct biometric of the client starting with one set then onto the next. Finally, the paper thought about a new application for CBAS related (conceivably) with changing point discovery calculations that don't require preparing information for both gate crasher and legitimate clients which can defeat the recognized confinements related with the current CBAS.

Tanmay Kumar Behera et al. [40] proposed the fact that the greater part of the extortion identification frameworks show great brings about recognizing fake exchanges, they additionally lead to the age of such a large number of bogus cautions. This accepts importance particularly in the space of charge card misrepresentation recognition where a charge card organization needs to limit its misfortunes at the same time, simultaneously, doesn't wish the cardholder to feel limited time after time. We have proposed a novel credit card misrepresentation location framework dependent on the reconciliation of two approaches that is fluffy bunching and neural system. We have utilized the fluffy c-implies grouping procedure for the gathering of the comparative datasets and utilized the neural organize as a learning procedure to decrease the misclassification rate dependent on the properties exchange sum, sort of things obtained, and time of exchange.

Imen Gaied et al. [41] have indicated that the neuro-fuzzy model is exceptionally strong for the decrease of bogus alerts and its higher exactness rate in examination with different models. The exchange of between superior and great understanding is troublesome and even incomprehensible: Data determination is a very significant resource to improve the consequences of our arrangement. Truth be told, our answer is justifiable through the security administrator with the Mamdani fluffy surmising framework which permits us to give phonetic principles. The errand of characterization is basic to segregate the wicked exercises of authentic exercises. On account of genuine positive; each sort of interruption is introduced by a solitary duplicate to decide the degree of assault that is done in a few steps.

Dr. Manish Shrivastava [42] has demonstrated that keystroke dynamics breaks down the way client types at a terminal by checking the console inputs a huge number of times each second, and points to recognize clients dependent on certain constant composing musicality designs. At the point when an individual kind, the latencies between progressive keystrokes, keystroke spans, finger position, and applied weight on the keys can be utilized to build a special mark for that person. For well-known, routinely composed strings, such marks can be very steady. The key focal point in applying console elements is that the device utilized right now framework, the console, is unpretentious and does not bring down one's work. Enlistment, as well as distinguishing proof, goes undetected by the client.

M.K. Sharma et al. [43] proposed quick and cross breed informal community investigation methods are required to mine feeling scores on informal communities as a gathering on the wrong conclusion may make issues for the general public or nation. Social network analysis (SNA) can be utilized as a significant apparatus for analysts, as the number of clients and gatherings expanding step by step on that social destinations, and an enormous gathering may impact others, yet the fundamental data is regularly appropriated and covered up on social site servers, so there is a need to structure some new methodologies for assortment and examination the social web information. Delicate processing systems, including fluffy sets, neural systems, hereditary calculations, harsh sets, and their hybridizations, have as of late been utilized to explain information mining issues. They endeavor to give rough arrangements at low cost, in this way accelerating the procedure. An order has been given dependent on the diverse delicate registering devices and their hybridizations utilized, the mining capacity executed, and the inclination rule chose by the model. Neuro-fuzzy hybridization abuses the qualities of both neural systems and fluffy sets in producing normal guidelines, taking care of uncertain and blended mode information, and demonstrating profoundly nonlinear choice limits. Space information, in a common structure, can be encoded in the system for improved execution.

John C. Stewart et al. [44] have come up with the exhibition of the keystroke biometric framework that is far better than that of the stylometry one. While the keystroke and stylometry biometrics are both social, they work at various psychological levels. The keystroke biometric works at basically a programmed engine control level. Stylometry, regardless, works at a higher subjective level, and because it includes word and linguistic structure level units, any longer content sections are expected comparative with those required by the keystroke biometric. To get framework execution right now mimicked the validation procedure of many genuine clients attempting to get verified and of numerous frauds attempting to get confirmed as different clients. A significant preferred position of this vector-distinction model is that it gives moderately enormous quantities of between and intra-individual separation tests. Even though test-taker verification continuously would not be conceivable with the depicted strategy because of the noteworthy measure of information required (half or full test), deferred validation with clump preparing ought to be adequate for college and HEOA prerequisites. Significant parameters in creation attribution strategies are the length and number of preparing and testing writings, and the number of potential writers. Another significant figure found in this stylometry study was the connection between the writings under investigation and how the writings are created. For instance, we found a moderately solid connection between the test responses and the test questions creating the appropriate responses.

P. Campisi et al. [45] proposed a keystroke elements-based validation strategy with application to cell phones, which can be utilized as a secret key solidifying component. In actuality, a solid secure verification framework can't depend on the sole keystroke elements, which anyway can be a module of an increasingly unpredictable framework, which can give, as essential security, a secret key based convention in the end solidified by keystroke investigation. Inside this situation, the client who needs to be verified needs both to type the right secret key and to utilize the authentic client's right composing example. In particular, we have researched the achievability of static content-based verification utilizing as information gadget mobile phone keypads the accomplished exhibitions are near those gotten utilizing other social biometrics, for instance, a client's mark. Additionally, the social acknowledgment of keystroke-based verification is very high, which, together with intriguing reachable execution, makes keystroke elements a decent contender to be utilized for secure confirmation utilizing mobile phones.

Arun Ross et al. [46] have come up with the confinements of the present condition of the biometric innovation ought not to be understood to suggest that it isn't as of now valuable in numerous applications. Truth be told, there is an enormous number of biometric arrangements that have been effectively conveyed to give helpful incentives in pragmatic applications. For instance, the hand geometry framework has filled in as a decent access control arrangement in numerous organizations, for example, college quarters, building passageways, and time and participation applications. AFIS systems have been giving staggering an incentive to society (since their commencement in the United States in the late 1960s), incorporating programmed and manual procedures. Disneyworld utilizes the finger geometry data of people to guarantee that a season pass isn't shared among different individual's further iterative patterns of innovation improvement, application to new areas, sensible execution assessment, and institutionalization efforts5 will encourage the pattern of manufacture. As biometric innovation develops, there will be expanding connections among the market, the advances, and the applications. This connection will be impacted by the extra worth of the innovation, client acknowledgment, and the believability of the administration supplier. It is too soon to anticipate precisely where and how biometric innovation will develop and into which specific applications it will get installed (see Table V for a rundown of potential applications). Yet it is sure that biometric-based acknowledgment will impact how we direct our day-by-day business due to the inborn potential for viably connecting individuals to records, in this way guaranteeing data security.

Rosy Vinayak et al. [47] have come up with the current study using keystroke dynamics as a form of two-factor biometric security. For a fruitful login into the framework, right off the bat secret word ought to be known, and also, composing design should coordinate Users don't regard these conditions as they feel them very exacting and hard to be applied. The answer to these issues is keystroke elements. Keystroke dynamics is a social biometric approach to improve the PC get to rights. It checks the individual by its keystroke composing design. Keystroke biometric depends on the presumption that the composing example of every client is remarkable. The target of this survey paper is to abridge the notable approaches utilized in keystroke elements.

Roman V. Yampolskiy [48] has come up with the most well-known conduct biometrics; however, any human conduct can be utilized as a reason for individual profiling and consequent confirmation. Some social biometrics which is rapidly making strides however are not a piece of this review incorporate profiling of shopping conduct dependent on showcase lolled examination (Prassas et al., 2001), web perusing and snap stream profiling (Fu and Shih, 2002; Goecks and Shavlik, 2000; Liang and Lai, 2002), and even TV inclinations (Democratic Media, 2001). Social biometrics are especially appropriate for confirmation of clients who connect with PCs, mobile phones, brilliant vehicles, or retail locations terminals. As the quantity of electronic machines utilized in homes and workplaces increments, so does the potential for use of this paper and promising innovation. Future research ought to be aimed at expanding by and large precision of such frameworks, e.g. by investigating the plausibility of creating multimodal social biometrics; as individuals regularly take part in numerous practices simultaneously, e.g. chatting on a PDA while driving or utilizing console and mouse simultaneously

Rohit A. Patil [49] has written a paper underscoring the significance of keystroke elements for work area, workstation, and so forth. The usage of keystroke elements in the work area is savvy and perfect as a combination of outer equipment isn't required. The finish of the paper depends on contrasting the information put away from a client with the login contribution for validation. Keystroke dynamics is a two-factor security biometric security, consequently, for a fruitful login, right off the bat secret phrase ought to be known and besides, composing beat ought to be coordinate. In human conduct security arrangement of any keypad requires making programming. In another strategy for biometrics, equipment is required yet human conduct technique we can create a safe key to ensure the secret phrase. This key is producing as indicated by human conduct for example at the point when the client gives a secret phrase he utilizes his composing pace to fill the secret word. The key is produced by programming to figure various occasions in a millisecond. The primary disadvantage of this task is various sorts of the console. In any case, if more work is done on this undertaking and discover the answer for that and can be the better progression of these keystroke elements. On the off chance that all consoles of the same style, the same high the lights are utilized then it gives better outcomes.

Yu Zhong et al. [50] has proposed that keystroke elements encourage a characteristic and financially savvy route for security and access security of PCs and cell phones. It additionally considers persistent validation by checking a client's composing conduct during the whole login session without any interference to the client's standard work. The utilization of consoles for individual distinguishing proof had been contemplated even before PCs were presented. It has been drawing in expanding consideration and interests as our expanding reliance on PCs and cell phones to store private and delicate data requests solid security assurance. Regardless of many years of research, keystroke elements examine is as yet advancing with many open challenges. Security applications. This exploration field faces the test regular to all other biometric modalities, for example, fingerprints and face acknowledgment, that is, how to perform heartily in certifiable situations with the nearness of different varieties. New include extraction and grouping techniques are still sought after. A combination of keystroke biometrics with other biometric modalities will give a definitive complete and secure confirmation arrangement.

Menal Dahiya [51] presented the work that depicts the helpfulness and strength of the Back Propagation neural system based secret phrase validation plot. The proposed verification conspire included two significant techniques: sign in and client approval. The system could review all the confirm clients precisely and dismissing the unapproved clients. The execution can be worked out for more clients.

Aleix Dorca Josa et al. [52] came up with the most significant result—that is, the legitimacy of setting information as a recognizable proof element. It has been demonstrated, utilizing an exceptionally unfriendly and genuine condition, that utilizing just straightforward factual strategies offers a generally excellent pace of precision, tantamount, if worse, to past examinations in comparable brutal situations. The outcomes got when utilizing consolidated tree models demonstrate that setting is significant to include. This outcome is profoundly significant to perform future research dependent on relevant data. The best word length result was to utilize all accessible word lengths. The best recursion technique isn't utilizing any recursion however just when sessions and models are of a certain quality. This is of principal significance and it affirms the significance of the situation of the letters and that not all data in a word ought to be dealt with similarly. It is smarter to have fewer data however of preferred quality over heaps of terrible data. When there are a base number of words found in the model, instead of tolerating any measured session to be looked at against the models, the outcomes are much better. This is in concordance with what different examinations have likewise expressed. The combination technique dependent on the proposed casting a ballot conspires consistently improves the outcomes when thought about to fractional gd esteems. From these, the weighted mean and the median measurement will in general be the ones that perform better.

Wendy Chen et al. [53] conducted research on keystroke elements biometrics has been expanding, particularly in the most recent decade. The primary inspiration driving this exertion is because of the way that keystrokes elements biometrics is prudent and can be effectively incorporated into the current PC security frameworks with insignificant modification and client intervention. Numerous examinations have been conducted in terms of information obtaining gadgets, including portrayals, classification methods, trial conventions, and assessments. Nonetheless, an exceptional broad overview and assessment aren't yet available. The goal of this paper is to give a sagacious study and correlation on keystroke elements biometrics examine performed all through the most recent three decades, just as offering recommendations and conceivable future explore headings.

Siti Fairuz Nurr Sadikan et al. [54] proposed that KDA encourages a financially savvy and basic route for verifying any PC application and gadgets. It likewise can ceaselessly screen a client's composing conduct for the whole session without interferences. Presently, KDA is still advancing because of its favorable circumstances and effortlessness. Therefore, this paper examined its idea, sorts of biometrics, and order. Furthermore, the various uses of keystroke elements and keystroke benchmarking datasets were additionally audited. It is prescribed that future work on KDA center around web-based figuring out how to improve the security of the web learning condition.

Romain Giot et al. [55] have indicated that regardless of whether there are existing and utilized measurements to think about biometrics frameworks, it isn't a simple assignment to think about investigations for the keystroke elements methodology. This is in part because of the way that there are not enough subtleties in the papers of writing. Another piece of the issue is that there isn't sufficient open keystroke elements database to test the calculations. A few databases were utilized in a few papers, however not utilized by other analysts or made freely accessible. Our commitment is the spreading of a keystroke elements database and an instrument permitting the formation of such sort of database. The sharing of these instruments will permit scientists to work with similar information, and give greater believability in the correlations of the unique techniques.

Shaimaa Hameed Shaker et al. [56] proposed the utilization of allout composing as an extra feature added as far as possible of the highlights vector builds the framework security. Complete composing adds irregularity to the features vector because of its far incentive from the other highlights' values. So includes vectors that are standardized to expel the inconsistency. Irregularity and standardization add unpredictability to the framework bringing about better security. In terms of exactness, like a keystroke elements authentication framework, the proposed framework confirms a client with 6% FAR and 24% FRR. From Table 3, one can see that these two rates speak to decreased qualities contrasted and the framework doesn't utilize PCA diminished highlights. The purpose behind the proposed system to accomplish this decreased rate is that it utilized PCA to diminish the planning highlights. Diminishing the highlights expels the redundant information so the subsequently decreased segments are uncorrelated with one another. Uncorrelated information expands the generalization capacity of the NN getting the hang of bringing about better characterization and less preparing time because the NN separates quicker to the ideal yield.

Jayashri Mittal et al. [57] proposed right now to be client agreeable and vigorous. The adjustments in human conduct attributes are represented by the retraining of the framework. The substitute strategy for check goes about as a preventive measure for impostors having comparable attributes of an authentic client. By and large, the framework can give a protected and invulnerable confirmation component. Keystroke biometrics is an exceptionally valuable instrument in verification. It conquers the disadvantages of the current frameworks and is progressively vigorous. The low arrangement cost and the need for the necessity of particular equipment make it simple to execute. Secret key verification as an independent framework may not give the necessary security, however, it very well may be reinforced by utilizing keystroke biometrics

Paulo Henrique Pisani et al. [58] proposed an interruption identification frameworks dependent on the client conduct that is a promising choice to control data fraud. Among the highlights to be dissected to characterize the client's conduct, this work considered a biometric innovation known as keystroke elements. The semi methodical audit we directed here might be used to control the future looks into right now. A precise audit includes a proper meaning of the survey convention before beginning the audit. Thus, the outcomes accomplished by the survey might be replicated by different examines as a way of approval. Here, the primary objective was to recognize the best in class in keystroke elements. To play out this assignment, this survey recognized focal points and impediments of the utilization of keystroke elements, highlights extricated from keystroke information, arrangement algorithms, ways of assessing the presentation, and datasets for benchmarking. A potential pattern in keystroke elements is its utilization in contact screen gadgets because of their expanding accessibility. These gadgets may give extra highlights to expand precision.

Fatma Taher et al. [59] discuss division forms that have been utilized. The first was Hopfield neural network (HNN) and the subsequent one was Fuzzy C-Mean (FCM) clustering calculation. It was discovered that the HNN division results are more exact and solid than FCM grouping in all cases. The HNN prevailing with regards to distinguishing and sectioning the cores and cytoplasm districts. Anyway, FCM flopped in identifying the cores, rather it identified just a piece of it. Notwithstanding that, the FCM isn't touchy to power varieties as the segmentation blunder at intermingling is bigger with FCM contrasted with that with HNN. Nonetheless, because of the extraordinary variety in the dim level and the relative complexity among the pictures which divides results less precise, we applied a standard-based thresholding classifier as a pre-preparing step. The sift holding classifier is prevailing with regards to taking care of the issue of in-strained quality variety and in recognizing the cores and cytoplasm areas, it can cover all the garbage cells and to decide the best rang of limit esteems. In general, the thresholding classifier has accomplished a decent precision of 98% with a high estimation of affectability and explicitness of 83% and 99% individually. The HNN will be utilized as a reason for a Computer-Aided Diagnosis (CAD) framework for early identification of lung disease. Later on, we intend to consider a Bayesian choice hypothesis for the discovery of the lung malignant growth cells, trailed by developing a model dependent on mean move calculation which joined edge recognition and an area-based way to deal with removing the homogeneous tissues spoke to in the picture.

Po-Ming Lee [60] has come up with three speculated connections between feelings and keystroke elements that are replied by utilizing conventional factual strategies of utilizing ML calculations. The proof found in the present investigation bolsters the speculations that keystroke term and inertness are affected by excitement, while neglected to demonstrate the guessed connection between the exactness pace of console composing and feelings (regardless of the way that the p-values for valence and excitement are both little). The discoveries of the present examination are normal to help the improvement in innovation that distinguishes clients' feeling through keystroke elements, which might be applied to different applications

5.3 Proposed Method

The proposed work combines password authentication with key-stroke dynamics/biometrics. It takes in the following parameters for authentication apart from the username and password:

1. Dwell time
2. Flight time
3. Usage of backspace
4. The overall time for typing

After storing the templates k nearest neighbor algorithm is used for classifying the input patterns at the time of login.

As shown in Figure 5.1, while entering into the authenticated credentials, the user will be able to access the data. If the user will not be able to use the credential, that means the user is not valid or maybe some other person is trying to steal the information from the user to get the personal detail or other important details.

Keystroke elements highlights are extricated in Figure 5.1 by breaking down the planning data of the key down/hold/up occasions. We will utilize three fundamental highlights press time (likewise

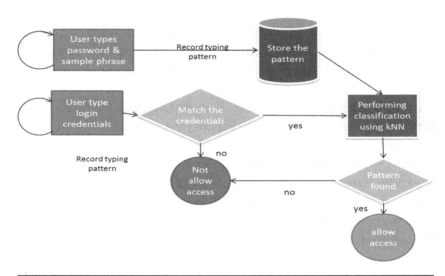

Figure 5.1: Password Authentication Using Data Mining.

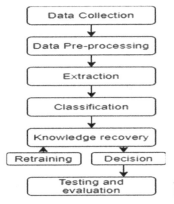

Figure 5.2: Data Abstraction from the Phases.

called stay time), between key time (additionally called flight time), and a complete time for our check procedure. The press time is the time interim between back to back key press and key discharge while the between key time is the time length in the middle of discharging a key and squeezing the following key. In Figure 5.2 this framework will store the keystroke times in correspondence to the client's other certification subtleties like username and the secret phrase in a database. The login stage happens at whatever point a client needs to get to the framework.

Before talking about the methodologies taken by analysts in keystroke elements, the highlights that can be seen in Figure 5.3 are extricated from the composing information, as portrayed here. While composing, the PC can record the time at which key is squeezed (stay time), to what extent the key is squeezed, and inertness between consecutive keys for example time slipped by from one key to a resulting key. The time estimated between the key up and the key

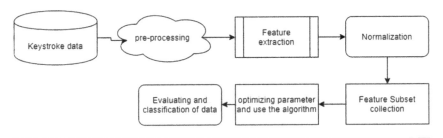

Figure 5.3: Normalization after the Extraction.

down is called flight time. Along these lines from the crude information, three planning highlights can be separated are press-to-press (PP), discharge to-discharge (RR), and discharge to-press (RP).

As seen in Figure 5.3, while entering into the classification we proposed calculation finds the contrast between real worth put away in the database and the current estimation of login client. Here, edge esteem is accepted to contrast and time. This edge esteems increment the effectiveness of the result. This worth is contrasted with the present time of login client if the worth will be coordinated by the edge esteem the individual is acknowledged or called a validated client. This worth will be changed by examination. Utilizing this yield FAR (false acknowledge proportion) and FRR (bogus reject ratio) values are determined.

Other planning data (see Figure 5.4) represents the time it takes to compose a word, digraph (two letters), or tri-diagram (three letters), which can likewise be extricated. Diagraph goes under press-to-press classification. Digraphs contain two successive keystrokes, while tri-charts contain three; this proceeds for any number of mixes, which makes n-diagrams of the hold time and key latency

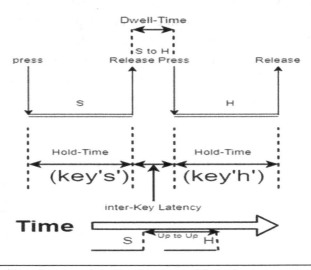

Figure 5.4: Time Latency of the Key Pressing and Releasing.

5.4 Conclusion

The keystroke element has made some amazing progress as a potential biometrics framework. Research on keystroke dynamics is going in a new way as the focus is given to contact gadgets. A great deal of work still should be done to make a functional biometrics application which will consider different varieties and precisely foresee if the client is legitimate or not. Being shoddy biometrics gives it a favorable position over other conventional biometrics. Furthermore, the way that it fills in as an additional layer of security in conjunction with knowledge-based validation like passwords makes it significantly more successful. In this study, we have attempted to outline keystroke dynamics to the best of our knowledge for specialists who are new to this investigation so they can work at promising research of their own.

References

1. Alshanketi F., Traoré I., and Ahmed A. A. "Improving Performance and Usability in Mobile Keystroke Dynamic Biometric Authentication." *2016 IEEE Security and Privacy Workshops (SPW)*, pp. 66–73, 2016.
2. Jaha F., and Kartit A. "Pseudo code of two-factor authentication for BYOD." *2017 International Conference on Electrical and Information Technologies (ICEIT)*, pp. 1–7, 2017.
3. Baynath P., Soyjaudah K. M., and Khan M. H. "Keystroke recognition using chaotic neural network." *2017 3rd Iranian Conference on Intelligent Systems and Signal Processing (ICSPIS)*, pp. 59–63, 2017.
4. Ferrari C., Marini D., and Moro M. "An Adaptive Typing Biometric System with Varying users Model." *2018 32nd International Conference on Advanced Information Networking and Applications Workshops (WAINA)*, pp. 564–568, 2018.
5. Chatterjee S., Roy S., Das A. K., Chattopadhyay S., Kumar N., and Vasilakos A. V. "Secure biometric-based authentication scheme using chebyshev chaotic map for multi-server environment." *IEEE Transactions on Dependable and Secure Computing*, vol. 15, no. 5, pp. 824–839, 2016.
6. Smriti P., Srivastava S., and Singh S. "Keyboard Invariant Biometric Authentication." *2018 4th International Conference on Computational Intelligence & Communication Technology (CICT)*, pp. 1–6, 2018.
7. Coakley M. J., Monaco J. V., and Tappert C. C. "Keystroke biometric studies with short numeric input on smartphones." *2016 IEEE 8th International Conference on Biometrics Theory, Applications and Systems (BTAS)*, pp. 1–6, 2016.
8. Ali M. L., Tappert C. C., Qiu M., and Monaco J. V. "Authentication and identification methods used in keystroke biometric systems." *2015 IEEE 17th International Conference on High Performance Computing and Communications, 2015 IEEE 7th International Symposium on Cyberspace Safety and Security, and 2015 IEEE 12th International Conference on Embedded Software and Systems*, pp. 1424–1429, IEEE, 2015.
9. Habib M., and Alqatawna J. "A Proposed Password-Free Authentication Scheme Based on a Hybrid Vein-Keystroke Approach." *2017 International Conference on New Trends in Computing Sciences (ICTCS)*, pp. 173–178, 2017.
10. Haque M. A., Khan N. Z., and Khatoon G. "Authentication through keystrokes: What you type and how you type." *2015 IEEE International Conference on Research in Computational Intelligence and Communication Networks (ICRCICN)*, pp. 257–261, 2015.
11. Shen S. S., Lin S. H., Kang T. H., and Chien W. "Enhanced keystroke dynamics authentication utilizing pressure detection." *2016 International Conference on Applied System Innovation (ICASI)*, pp. 1–4, IEEE, 2016.
12. Can Y. S., and Alagöz F. "User identification using Keystroke Dynamics." *2014 22nd Signal Processing and Communications Applications Conference (SIU)*, pp. 1083–1085, IEEE, 2014.

13. Baynath P., Soyjaudah K. S., and Khan M. H. M. "Keystroke recognition using neural network." *2017 5th International Symposium on Computational and Business Intelligence (ISCBI)*, pp. 86–90, IEEE, 2017, August.

14. Jadhav C., Kulkarni S., Shelar S., Shinde K., and Dharwadkar N. V. "Biometrie authentication using keystroke dynamics." *2017 International Conference on I-SMAC (IoT in Social, Mobile, Analytics and Cloud) (I-SMAC)*, pp. 870–875, IEEE, 2017.

15. Pramana M. I., Suhardi, Kurniawan N. B., and Sembiring J. "Keystroke dynamics for authentication using dynamic time warping." *2017 14th International Joint Conference on Computer Science and Software Engineering (JCSSE)*, pp. 1–5, 2017.

16. Huang J., Hou D., Schuckers S., Law T., and Sherwin A. "Benchmarking keystroke authentication algorithms." *2017 IEEE Workshop on Information Forensics and Security (WIFS)*, pp. 1–6, IEEE, 2017.

17. Dwivedi C., Kalra D., Naidu D., and Aggarwal S. "Keystroke dynamics based biometric authentication: A hybrid classifier approach." *2018 IEEE Symposium Series on Computational Intelligence (SSCI)*, pp. 266–273, IEEE, 2018.

18. Ali M. L., and Tappert C. C. "POHMM/SVM: A Hybrid Approach for Keystroke Biometric User Authentication." *2018 IEEE International Conference on Real-time Computing and Robotics (RCAR)*, pp. 612–617, 2018.

19. Handa J., Singh S., and Saraswat S. "A comparative study of Mouse and Keystroke Based Authentication." *2019 9th International Conference on Cloud Computing, Data Science & Engineering (Confluence)*, pp. 670–674, IEEE, 2019.

20. Giri D., Sherratt R. S., and Maitra T. "A novel and efficient session spanning biometric and password based three-factor authentication protocol for consumer USB Mass Storage Devices." *IEEE Transactions on Consumer Electronics*, vol. 62, pp. 283–291, 2016.

21. Chandrasekar V. "User authentication based on hausdroff distance in keystroke dynamics using memetic algorithms." *International Journal of Pure and Applied Mathematics*, vol. 118, no. 14, pp. 117–125, 2018.

22. Wu J., and Chen Z. "An implicit identity authentication system considering changes of gesture based on keystroke behaviors." *International Journal of Distributed Sensor Networks*, vol. 11, no. 6, p.470274, 2015.

23. Salem A., and Obaidat M. S. "A novel security scheme for behavioral authentication systems based on keystroke dynamics." *Security and Privacy*, vol. 2, no. 2, p.e64, 2019.

24. Honggui H., Ying L., and Junfei Q. "A fuzzy neural network approach for online fault detection in waste water treatment process." *Computers & Electrical Engineering*, vol. 40, no. 7, pp. 2216–2226, 2014.

25. Shen C., Yu T., Xu H., Yang G., and Guan X. "User practice in password security: An empirical study of real-life passwords in the wild." *Computers & Security*, vol. 61, pp. 130–141, 2016.

26. Nimbhorkar, N. M. A. P. S. "A survey paper on continuous authentication by multimodal biometric." *International Journal of Advanced Research in Computer Engineering & Technology (IJARCET)*, vol. 4, no. 11, 2015.

27. Buchoux A., and Clarke N. L. "Deployment of Keystroke Analysis on a Smartphone." 2008.

28. Alsultan A., and Warwick K. "Keystroke dynamics authentication: a survey of free-text methods." *International Journal of Computer Science Issues (IJCSI)*, vol. 10, no. 4, p.1, 2013.

29. Chourasia N. Authentication of the user by keystroke dynamics for banking transaction system. In *Proceedings of International Conference on Advances in Engineering & Technology*, pp. 41–45, 2014.

30. Karim N. A., and Shukur Z. "Review of user authentication methods in online examination." 2015.

31. Epp C., Lippold M., and Mandryk R. L. "Identifying emotional states using keystroke dynamics." In *Proceedings of the sigchi conference on human factors in computing systems*, pp. 715–724, 2011.

32. Giot R., El-Abed M., and Rosenberger C. "Web-based benchmark for keystroke dynamics biometric systems: A statistical analysis." In *2012 Eighth International Conference on Intelligent Information Hiding and Multimedia Signal Processing*, pp. 11–15, IEEE, 2012.

33. Casey K. "Using Keystroke Analytics to Improve Pass-Fail Classifiers." 2017.

34. BrajeshSingh S. S., Shah Y., and Singh V. "Literature survey on keystroke dynamics for user authentication." *International Journal on Recent and Innovation Trends in Computing and Communication*, vol. 5, no. 5, pp. 280–282, 2017.

35. Teh P. S., Teoh A. B. J., and Yue S. "A survey of keystroke dynamics biometrics." *The Scientific World Journal, 2013*, 2013.

36. Shepherd S. J. "Continuous authentication by analysis of keyboard typing characteristics." 1995.

37. Allen L. K., Mills C., Jacovina M. E., Crossley S., D'mello S., and McNamara D. S. "Investigating boredom and engagement during writing using multiple sources of information: the essay, the writer, and keystrokes." In *Proceedings of the Sixth International Conference on Learning Analytics & Knowledge*, pp. 114–123, 2016.

38. Sim T., and Janakiraman R. "Are Digraphs Good for Free-Text Keystroke Dynamics?" *2007 IEEE Conference on Computer Vision and Pattern Recognition*, pp. 1–6, 2007.

39. Solami E. A., Boyd C., Clark A. J., and Islam A. K. "Continuous Biometric Authentication: Can It Be More Practical?" *2010 IEEE 12th International Conference on High Performance Computing and Communications (HPCC)*, pp. 647–652, 2010.

40. Behera T. K., and Panigrahi S. "Credit card fraud detection: a hybrid approach using fuzzy clustering & neural network." In *2015 Second International Conference on Advances in Computing and Communication Engineering*, pp. 494–499, IEEE, 2015.

41. Gaied I., Jemili F., and Korbaa O. "Intrusion detection based on neuro-fuzzy classification." In *2015 IEEE/ACS 12th International Conference of Computer Systems and Applications (AICCSA)*, pp. 1–8, IEEE, 2015.
42. Shrivastava M. "Password Authentication Method Using Keystroke Biometric." *Journal Of Computing*, vol. 3, no. 6, pp. 125–129, 2011.
43. Kumar R., and Sharma M. "Advanced neuro-fuzzy approach for social media mining methods using cloud." *International Journal of Computer Applications*, vol. 975, p.8887, 2016.
44. Stewart J. C., Monaco J. V., Cha S. H., and Tappert C. C. "An investigation of keystroke and stylometry traits for authenticating online test takers." In *2011 International Joint Conference on Biometrics (IJCB)*, pp. 1–7, IEEE, 2011.
45. Campisi P., Maiorana E., Bosco M. L., and Neri A. "User authentication using keystroke dynamics for cellular phones." *IET Signal Processing*, vol. 3, no. 4, pp. 333–341, 2009.
46. Jain A. K., Ross A., and Pankanti S. "Biometrics: a tool for information security." *IEEE Transactions on Information Forensics and Security*, vol. 1, pp. 125–143, 2006.
47. Vinayak R., and Arora K. "A survey of user authentication using keystroke dynamics." *International Journal of Scientific Research Engineering & Technology (IJSRET)*, vol. 4, no. 4, pp. 378–384, 2015.
48. Yampolskiy R. V., and Govindaraju V. "Behavioural biometrics: a survey and classification." *International Journal of Biometrics*, vol. 1, no. 1, pp. 81–113, 2008.
49. Patil R. A., and Renke A. L. "Keystroke dynamics for user authentication and identification by using typing rhythm." *International Journal of Computer Applications*, vol. 144, no. 9, pp. 27–33, 2016.
50. Zhong Y., and Deng Y. "A survey on keystroke dynamics biometrics: approaches, advances, and evaluations." *Recent Advances in User Authentication Using Keystroke Dynamics Biometrics*, pp. 1–22, 2015.
51. Dahiya M. "User Authentication Mechanism Based on Neural Networks Menal Dahiya." 2016.
52. Josa A. D., Moreno J. A. M., and Pérez E. S. "Using Keystroke Dynamics and context features to assess authorship in online learning environments."
53. Chen W., and Chang W. "Applying hidden Markov models to keystroke pattern analysis for password verification." In *Proceedings of the 2004 IEEE International Conference on Information Reuse and Integration, 2004. IRI 2004.*, pp. 467–474, 2004.
54. Sadikan S. F. N., Ramli A. A., and Fudzee M. F. M. "A survey paper on keystroke dynamics authentication for current applications." In *AIP Conference Proceedings*, vol. 2173, no. 1, p.020010, 2019.
55. Giot R., El-Abed M., and Rosenberger C. "Greyc keystroke: a benchmark for keystroke dynamics biometric systems." In *2009 IEEE 3rd International Conference on Biometrics: Theory, Applications, and Systems*, pp. 1–6, 2009.

56. Shaker S. H., Saydani R. J., and Obaid M. K. "Keystroke Dynamics Authentication based on Principal Component Analysis and Neural Network." 2014.

57. D'lima N., and Mittal J. "Password authentication using keystroke biometrics." In *2015 International conference on communication, information & computing technology (ICCICT)*, pp. 1–6, 2015.

58. Pisani P. H., and Lorena A. C. "A systematic review on keystroke dynamics." *Journal of the Brazilian Computer Society*, vol. 19, no. 4, pp. 573–587, 2013.

59. Taher F., and Sammouda R. "Lung cancer detection by using artificial neural network and fuzzy clustering methods." In *2011 IEEE GCC Conference and Exhibition (GCC)*, pp. 295–298, IEEE, 2011.

60. Lee P. M., Tsui W. H., and Hsiao T. C. "The influence of emotion on keyboard typing: an experimental study using auditory stimuli." *PloS one*, vol. 10, no. 6, 2015.

6

HEALTHCARE DATA ANALYTICS OVER BIG DATA

E. HARI AND H. PARVEEN SULTANA

Research Scholar, VIT, Vellore,
Tamil Nandu
VIT, Vellore, Tamil Nandu

Contents

6.1 Introduction

The healthcare industry historically generates a large amount of data driven by record keeping, compliance and regulatory requirements, and patient care. Most of the data used to be stored in hard copies: log forms, reports, and patient details. At present, the current trend is moving towards digitalization, where we are having a huge amount of data which focuses on the mandatory requirements and also the potential to improve the quality of healthcare data by reducing the cost. When you generate this kind of massive amount of data, this will hold all the ranges of medical and healthcare functions like disease surveillance, clinical decision support, and population health management. This massive amount of data will lead to form called "Big Data."

The concept of Big Data in healthcare is getting popular not only because of its volume but also because of the different types of data types and the speed at which it must be managed. In general, Big Data in healthcare consist of clinical data, patient data in electronic patient records (EPRs), machine generated, and sensor data. Healthcare organizations and other stakeholders in the healthcare delivery system might develop more carefully and insightful diagnoses and treatments, which would result in higher-quality care at lower costs and in better outcomes overall.

6.1.1 Introduction to Big Data Analytics in Healthcare

Over the next few years, the volume of healthcare data is expected to grow dynamically. In addition to this, healthcare restitution models are changing drastically. Although profit is not a primary factor for healthcare organizations, it is highly important to acquire the available tools, infrastructure, and techniques to leverage Big Data effectively or else risk losing potentially millions of dollars in revenue and profits.

Big Data "consist of a large volume of high velocity and volatile data that require advanced techniques and technologies to enable the capture, storage, distribution, management and analysis of the information" [3,19]. These properties all will be satisfied by the healthcare data, so we are using Big Data technology.

6.1.2 The V's Directly Associated with Healthcare Data

The data analytics associated with big data are described by the following characteristics like:

- Volume
- Velocity and
- Variety

And also the health-related data will be generated and accumulated continuously, which results in an incredible volume of data. The already generated volume of existing healthcare data consist of personal medical records, radiology images, clinical trial data submitted to the Food and Drug Administration (FDA) [3], human genetics and population data genomic sequences, etc., and also new types of Big Data such as 3D imaging, genomics, and biometric sensor readings, are also fueling this exponential growth of healthcare data analytics. The reason behind this growing complexity or abundance in healthcare data is because standard medical practice [4] is moving from relatively ad-hoc and subjective decision-making to evidence-based healthcare and more incentives to professionals/hospitals to use electronic health record (EHR) technology.

6.2 Data Sources Used for Healthcare Data Analytics

Development of new technologies such as capturing devices, sensors, and mobile applications will also contribute a huge volume of data. At the same time, collection of genomic information has also become cheaper, patient social communications in digital forms are increasing, and more medical knowledge/discoveries are being accumulated.

6.2.1 Overall Goals of Big Data Analytics in Healthcare

- Take advantage of the massive amounts of data and provide the right intervention to the right patient at the right time [6].
- Provide personalized care to the patient at every instance.
- Potentially benefit all the components of a healthcare system, which include provider, payer, patient, and management.
- Introduce healthcare analysts and practitioners to the advancements in the computing field to effectively handle and make inferences from voluminous and heterogeneous healthcare data.

6.2.2 Challenges in Healthcare Data Analytics

The list of challenges with analyzing healthcare data [1] include the following:

- Inferring knowledge from complex heterogeneous patient sources and leveraging the patient/data correlations in longitudinal records.
- Understanding unstructured clinical notes in the right context.
- Efficiently handling large volumes of medical imaging data and extracting potentially useful information and biomarkers.
- Analyzing genomic data is a computationally intensive task, and combining with standard clinical data adds layers of complexity.
- Capturing the patient's behavioral data through several sensors: their various social interactions and communications.
- Some of the online patient/caregiver support systems like CancerCompass and PatientsLikeMe allow patients and humanitarians to post health-related questions. In such situations,

there is a significant volume of repetitive questions. One of the possible reasons for such repetition could be that as forums grow longer, patients and humanitarians do not have sufficient time or patience to read through all previous questions before posting their own question. The main challenge from this is to design and implement a system that gives questions by identifying a maximum of two or three existing questions which are most similar to it.

So by observing all of these challenges with reference to healthcare data, we will get a conclusion that analyzing and giving the most suitable information is very important.

6.2.3 Challenges Related to IoT Security

The following are the top ten challenges for IoT security:

- Secure constrained devices
- Authorize and authenticate devices
- Manage device updates
- Secure communication
- Ensure data privacy and integrity
- Secure web, mobile, and cloud applications
- Ensure high availability
- Detect vulnerabilities and incidents
- Manage vulnerabilities
- Predict and preempt security issues

6.2.3.1 Secure Constrained Devices Many IoT devices have limited amounts of storage, memory, and processing capability, and they often need to be able to operate on lower power, for example, when running on batteries. Security approaches that rely heavily on encryption are not a good fit for these constrained devices, because they are not capable of performing complex encryption and decryption quickly enough to be able to transmit data securely in real time. These devices are often vulnerable to side-channel attacks, such as power analysis attacks, that can be used to reverse-engineer these algorithms. Instead, constrained devices typically only employ fast, lightweight encryption algorithms. Internet of Things (IoT) systems should make use of multiple layers of defense, for example, segregating devices onto separate networks and using firewalls, to compensate for these device limitations.

6.2.3.2 Authorize and Authenticate Devices   With so many devices offering potential points of failure within an IoT system, device authentication and authorization is critical for securing IoT systems. Devices must establish their identity before they can access gateways and upstream services and apps. However, many IoT devices fall down when it comes to device authentication, for example, by using weak basic password authentication or using passwords unchanged from their default values.

Adopting an IoT platform that provides security by default helps to resolve these issues, for example, by enabling two-factor authentication (2FA) and enforcing the use of strong passwords or certificates. IoT platforms also provide device authorization services used to determine which services, apps, or resources each device has access to throughout the system.

6.2.3.3 Manage Device Updates   Applying updates, including security patches, to firmware or software that runs on IoT devices and gateways presents a number of challenges. For example, you need to keep track of updates that are available to apply consistently across distributed environments with heterogeneous devices that communicate through a range of different networking protocols. Not all devices support over-the-air updates or updates without downtime, so devices might need to be physically accessed or temporarily pulled from production to apply updates.

Also, updates might not be available for all devices, particularly older devices or those devices that are no longer supported by their manufacturer. Even when updates are available, the owners of a device might opt out of applying an update. As part of your device management, you need to keep track of the versions that are deployed on each device and which devices are candidates for retirement after updates are no longer available. Device manager systems often support pushing out updates automatically to devices, as well as managing rollbacks if the update process fails. They can also help to ensure that only legitimate updates are applied, for example, through the use of digital signing.

6.2.3.4 Secure Communication   Once the devices themselves are secured, the next IoT security challenge is to ensure that communication across the network between devices and cloud services or apps is secure. Many IoT devices don't encrypt messages before sending them over the network. However, best practice is to use transport encryption and to adopt standards like Transport Layer Secutiry (TLS). Using separate networks to isolate devices also helps with establishing secure, private communication so that data transmitted remain confidential.

6.2.3.5 Ensure Data Privacy and Integrity   It is also important that wherever the data end up after they have been transmitted across the network, they are stored and processed securely. Implementing data privacy includes redacting or anonymizing sensitive data before they are stored or using data separation to decouple personally identifiable information from IoT data payloads. Data that are no longer required should be disposed of securely, and if data are stored, maintaining compliance with legal and regulatory frameworks is also an important challenge. Ensuring data integrity may involve employing checksums or digital signatures to ensure data have not been modified. Blockchain, as a decentralized distributed ledger for IoT data, offers a scalable and resilient approach for ensuring the integrity of IoT data.

6.2.3.6 Secure Web, Mobile, and Cloud Applications   Web, mobile, and cloud apps and services are used to manage, access, and process IoT devices and data, so they must also be secured as part of a multi-layered approach to IoT security.

When developing IoT applications, be sure to apply secure engineering practices to avoid vulnerabilities such as the OWASP Top Ten vulnerabilities. Just like devices, apps should also support secure authentication, both for the apps themselves and the users of the applications, by providing options such as 2FA and secure password recovery options.

6.2.3.7 Ensure High Availability   As we come to rely more on IoT within our day-to-day lives, IoT developers must consider the availability of IoT data and the web and mobile apps that rely on that data, as well as our access to the physical things managed by IoT systems. The potential for disruption as a result of connectivity outages or device failures, or arising as a result of attacks like denial of service, is more than just an inconvenience.

In some applications, the impact of the lack of availability could mean loss of revenue, damage to equipment, or even loss of life. For example, in connected cities, IoT infrastructure is responsible for essential services such as traffic control, and in healthcare, IoT devices include pacemakers and insulin pumps. To ensure high availability, IoT devices must be protected against cyber-attacks as well as physical tampering. IoT systems must include redundancy to eliminate single points of failure and should also be designed to be resilient and fault tolerant so that they can adapt and recover quickly when problems do arise.

6.2.3.8 Detect Vulnerabilities and Incidents Despite best efforts, security vulnerabilities and breaches are inevitable. How do you know if your IoT system has been compromised? In large-scale IoT systems, the complexity of the system in terms of the number of devices connected and the variety of devices, apps, services, and communication protocols involved can make it difficult to identify when an incident has occurred. Strategies for detecting vulnerabilities and breaches include monitoring network communications and activity logs for anomalies, engaging in penetration testing and ethical hacking to expose vulnerabilities, and applying security intelligence and analytics to identify and notify when incidents occur.

6.2.3.9 Manage Vulnerabilities The complexity of IoT systems also makes it challenging to assess the repercussions of vulnerability or the extent of a breach in order to manage its impact. Challenges include identifying which devices were affected, what data or services were accessed or compromised, and which users were impacted, and then taking actions to resolve the situation. Device managers maintain a registry of devices, which can be used to temporarily disable or isolate affected devices until they can be patched. This feature is particularly important for key devices such as gateway devices in order to limit their potential to cause harm or disruption, for example, by flooding the system with fake data if they have been compromised. Actions can be applied automatically using a rules engine with rules based on vulnerability management policies.

6.2.3.10 Predict and Preempt Security Issues A longer-term IoT security challenge is to apply security intelligence not only for detecting and mitigating issues as they occur but also to predict and proactively protect against potential security threats. Threat modeling is one approach used to predict security issues. Other approaches include applying monitoring and analytics tools to correlate events and visualize unfolding threats in real time, as well as applying artificial intelligence (AI) to adaptively adjust security strategies applied based on the effectiveness of previous actions.

6.3 Methods for Using Healthcare Data Analytics

Doing any kind of analysis will start with data collection. The data collection process in a healthcare system can present many problems. Particularly, effective integration and effective forms of various healthcare data over a period of time can answer many of the impending healthcare problems.

General data collection and analysis can be diagrammatically represented, as shown in Figure 6.1. Here the admin is going to maintain all types of data, and they are only having the provision to access it from the sources. The EHR [2,20] database is going to act as our Big Data platform.

The EHR data are the core part of data analytics. And this is also going to become the best data source to maintain the information about healthcare, as given in Figure 6.2. All EHRs are maintained on a timely basis to produce analytical information based on the statistical models; these can also be used in doing research on the existing healthcare data.

In clinical terminology, the EHR data can be divided into two ways, namely,

- Structured EHR data
- Unstructured EHR data

The structured EHR data will use the data elements that are documenting patient information using controlled vocabulary

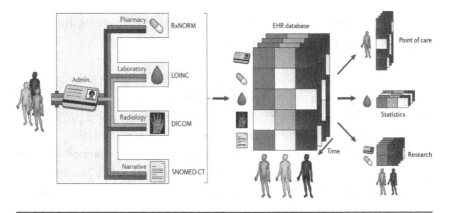

Figure 6.1 The Process of Data Collection and Analytics of Healthcare Data.

rather than the narrative process of the text. The historic insufficiency of structured data and standardization in the healthcare industry today causes a problem when sharing the content between providers.

Unstructured data in healthcare is a kind of information that typically requires a human touch to read, capture, and interpret properly. This kind of capturing includes machine-written and handwritten information on unstructured paper forms, audio voice dictations, email messages and attachments, and typed transactions.

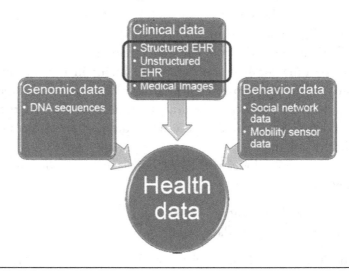

Figure 6.2 The Data Representation of EHR in the Healthcare System.

Any kind of unstructured data in healthcare will be brought into the EHR flow using the technical components of electronic document management systems (EDMS), including:

- The automated forms of classification and data capture systems
- Document management systems for version control, check-in/check-out, and security
- Maintaining eForms for online data entry and data collection
- Using records management technology to get controlled access to records and retain or destroy records in accordance with state regulations

In addition to the structured and unstructured EHR, ICD (International Classification of Disease) codes are also going to generate a huge volume of data.

6.3.1 The Role of ICD Codes in the Generation of Big Healthcare Data

ICD is a hierarchical terminology of diseases, signs, symptoms, and procedure codes maintained by the World Health Organization (WHO). In the United States most of the people are using ICD-9 and the rest of the world uses ICD-10. And also the rise of EMRs has led to the propagation of observational studies which are helpful to examine the preoperative period in terms of huge numbers; this is also one of the main reasons to produce Big Data. The work of Thomas et al. [4] falls short of invalidating codes for toxemia, since the authors did not investigate the exactness of coding, but rather looked at their use over time. Thus, it is unclear what is responsible for the discrepancy that they discovered, and it could be that coding for sepsis became more accurate over time.

6.3.2 Analyzing the ICD Codes and EHR Data

In general the term Big Data is not subjected to MeSH (Medical Subject Heading) – it is embodied by the MeSH in terms of "automatic data processing," "electronic data processing," "data mining," and "EHRs". However, it's very important to do some analytics on such type of data. Table 6.1 gives an idea about the terms associated with healthcare and how to query the results from Big Data.

Table 6.1   Frequent Terms Used in the Statistical Model of Data Analytics in Healthcare

CATEGORY	QUERY TERMS	CATEGORY	QUERY TERMS
• EHR	• Electronic Health Records • Electronic Medical Records* • Personal Health Records	• Privacy and Security	• Access Control* • Confidentiality • Consent • Patient Data Privacy • Data Sharing • Privacy • Privacy Mechanism* • Computer Security
• Data Analysis	• Artificial Intelligence • Big Data* • Cloud Computing* • Data Mining • Data Interpretation • Computer Simulation • Predictive Model* • Statistical Model • Visualization	• NLP	• Controlled Vocabulary • De-Identification* • Information Extraction • Information Storage and Retrieval • Knowledge Representation • Natural Language Processing • Text Mining
• Health Information Technology	• Clinical Decision Support System • Monitoring* • Quality Improvement • Social Media	• Translational Informatics	• Surveillance • Pharma covigilance • Phenotyping*

In general, a predictive model is a widely used buzzword in healthcare data analytics, which is applicable for "data visualization." Data visualization is critical for interpreting study outcomes, and this technique helps clinicians accept new methods. Visualization monitoring is also a broad concept, which also includes drug monitoring, patient monitoring, etc. "Access control" is also one of the new and popular topics in patient data privacy research. From Table 6.1, we have to specifically mention a technique called natural language processing (NLP), which is one of the core technologies employed in biomedical informatics. NLP can be used to analyze a large amount of data which consist of discharge summaries in an unstructured format. Therefore, using a technique like NLP can lead to extracting and structuring this descriptive information. This procedure can be treated as an important step in many EHR data secondary-use studies. By augmenting the amount of computable data, NLP can also help to address some aspects of incomplete data.

NLP starts with extracting the information from trivial data sources, namely ADEs from EHR data. Information extraction (IE) is a traditional area in which NLP is used to identify and classify name entities and relations from narrative text, like discharge summaries and prescriptions. Identifying the relations (relation identification) is the most promising field in IE, though we have many obstacles. In IE and RI we focus on

- Co-reference identification and
- Temporal relation extraction

The role of co-reference resolution is to recognize two mentions that refer to the same entity in a sentence or across sentences. Present co-reference resolution studies use the rule-based machine learning and hybrid systems to identify noun phrases, including person, pronoun, and concepts such as medical tests. In this method, the data quality will decide the performance of the systems.

Temporal relation extraction is also one of the methods in the information extraction process; it focuses on research direction because it is used to identify the complications, patient outcome predictions, and ADE detection. Previously, temporal relation was also utilized in the abstraction of emergency department (ED) computed tomography (CT) imaging reports. In addition to the NLP, we also using the data application and integration mechanism in EHR data to utilize and retrospectively assess treatment effectiveness in real-world settings, quality of care, and cost. A clinical decision support system (CDSS) helps to do multitasking on healthcare Big Data to make quick decisions.

A conceptual model for analyzing the Big Data in standard platforms is shown in Figure 6.3. The same can be applied to the healthcare data by dividing it into the following two categories: basic

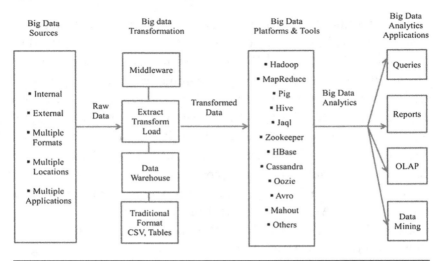

Figure 6.3 An Applied Conceptual Model for Big Data Analytics.

analytics and advanced analytics. The different platforms we used in the earlier architecture will be helpful to migrate the healthcare data into a general structured format to understand quickly. Now we will start the actual analytics part of the healthcare data with the basic analytics section.

6.3.3 Basic Analytics on Healthcare Data

It seems that the cost of healthcare has been consistently rising, at the same time the quality of care provided to the patients in some countries has not seen considerable improvements. In this section, we'll try to focus on the quality improvements in healthcare data by doing some basic analytics using sources available. Generally, the different forms of patient data can be stored in EHRs and biomedical images, which we discussed earlier. Here the basic analytics includes the techniques for mining the various sensor data and also biomedical signal analysis. In this part, we are specifically going to be brief about in-hospital clinical data, biomedical literature, and the behavioral data captured through social mediums. The list of analytics is as follows:

- Biomedical image analysis
- Sensor data analysis
- Biomedical signal analysis

- Genomic data analysis
- Clinical text mining
- Mining biomedical literature
- Social media analysis

6.3.3.1 Biomedical Image Analysis Today's medical imaging [9] plays a vital role in modern healthcare because of its immense capability in providing high-quality images of anatomical structures in human bodies. If we do the effective analysis of such type of images, the results will be useful for clinicians and medical researchers because it proves disease monitoring, treatment planning, and prognosis. We are using these biomedical images in magnetic resonance imaging (MRI), ultrasound (U/S), computed tomography (CT), and positron emission tomography (PET). Biomedical images provide a facility to look at and observe organs in the human body without hurting; this has tremendous implications on human health. By using these techniques, physicians are able to have a better understanding of an illness or other abnormal conditions without hurting or cutting the human body. The ultimate goal of analyzing a biomedical image is to generate quantitative information and make inferences from the sample images that can provide far more insights into a medical condition.

Now coming to the challenges we are facing in biomedical image analytics; the images we are using sometimes are varied, complex, and irregular shapes with some noisy values. The parts of biomedical image processing include object detection, image segmentation, feature extraction, and image registration.

6.3.3.2 Sensor Data Analysis Sensors in the medical field will be treated as ubiquitous in nature for both real-time and retrospective analysis of data. Various forms of medical data collection measures such as electroencephalogram (EEG, and electrocardiogram (ECG) are essentially sensors which are collecting signals from different parts in the human body. All the collected data instruments are frequently used for both retrospective analysis and real-time analysis. The best example of real-time analysis is observing and analyzing the intensive care unit (ICU) data and real-time remote monitoring patients with specific medical conditions. In all of these cases, the data volume will always increase to form Big Data. Consider an example of an ICU; it is very common for the sensor to receive data from various data sources that triggered the alarm in real time. Hence, it becomes an extremely important data model to analyze the sensor in health systems. These kinds of analytical methods are not only allowed for patients' physiological signals but also help to provide situational help to the bedside in intensive care.

6.3.3.3 Biomedical Signal Analysis   The process of measuring the signals from biological sources is called biological signal analysis; the origins of this process will lie in various kinds of physiological processes. Some of the best examples of such signals are electroneurogram (ENG), ECG, electromyogram (EMG), EEG, phonocardiogram (PCG), and so on. Biomedical signal analysis results will help us to diagnose the pathological and unexpected conditions in deciding a suitable care pathway. Biomedical signals can be single or continuous, depending upon the severity of the pathological condition. The problem associated with the biomedical signals is that they have a low signalto-noise ratio (SNR) and also the interdependency of the physiological systems. This problem occurs due to the fact that medical instruments can be noisy and it also requires preprocessing.

To overcome all the problems with data pre-processing and filtering techniques, we may apply dimensionality reduction techniques like principal component analysis (PCA), wavelet transformation, and singular value decomposition (SVD). Apart from all these techniques, we are also using time series analysis on signal data to visualize the variations of behavior with respect to time.

6.3.3.4 Genomic Data Analysis   A significant number of diseases are genetic in nature, with an example like genetic markers that lead an individual to be prone to diabetes [15], but these are still unknown. One more example of blindness caused by Stargardt disease is also genetic in nature. Here we'll try to understand the relationship between genetic markers, mutations, and disease conditions that have significant potential in supporting the development of different gene therapies to cure these conditions. The transformation process of genetic discoveries into personalized medicine practice is a highly nontrivial task with a lot of unresolved challenges.

Recent improvements have made the biotechnologies to generate a huge volume of data and medical information. So concentrating on such data will give eminent results to improve the genomic data.

6.3.3.5 Clinical Text Mining Clinical text mining is a process of extracting useful information from the clinical notes generated by hospitals about the patients. These types of notes will always be in an unstructured data format, and this is the backbone of most of the healthcare data. A few examples include transcription of dictations, direct entry by providers, or use of mobile applications to do speech recognition – all such data comes under the heading of unexploited information. The only source for analyzing this free text is a manual encoding approach because it is a costly and time-consuming process. It also becomes hard due to its complexity, unstructured nature, and heterogeneity.

To overcome all the problems and to improve the analytics approach, we move our process towards an advanced language processing mechanism called NLP, which was mentioned earlier.

6.3.3.6 Mining Biomedical literature Literature data have its own significance in the healthcare sector. As technology grows rapidly, the applications we are using for gathering biomedical literature has also increased. These applications will be acting as evidence for Big Data in healthcare. Mining these literature data will produce prevention, accessibility, and usability of digitally available resources that are important in biomedical applications.

Traditional data mining techniques and tools offer new knowledge discovery methods on biomedical data to extract, analyze, combine, and summarize textual data. With regard to challenging issues in biomedical text mining, we have some problems with the data because of their multidisciplinary nature in the fields. The mining literature approach brings some other benefits to biomedical research by linking textual evidence to biomedical pathways. This linking will reduce the cost of expert knowledge validation and generate a different hypothesis.

6.3.3.7 Social Media Analysis   Social media can also be widely used in the healthcare industry to get opinions and frequently asked questions from the general public to predict or to diagnose a disease. In this process, online communities provide a wealth of information about various aspects of healthcare. Social media data can be mined for basically pattern recognition and knowledge that make useful inferences about the population health and general public health monitoring system. It seems that most individual information on disease in social media posts and messages contain little information value, but when we aggregate all the individual posts and messages, it forms a huge volume of data. Extracting and analyzing such kind of data will always give the most promising results on the outcomes and predictive suggestions about a disease.

6.3.4 Advanced Data Analytics for Healthcare

To do some advanced data analytics, it is better to use a standard platform for processing the data and to visualize the large-scale contents. Here we'll try to design a standard platform for pre-processing and analyze the biomedical data.

Data analytics process (see Figure 6.4) will start with information extraction in any of the streams. In the healthcare data analytics sector, the information extraction is initiated from all the data gathering mediums like EHRs and different sensors used. After gathering the data, next step is to initiate extracting all the useful features from the available data to perform meaningful analysis. Upon generating such kind of analysis, the final stage is to propose a predictive model for forecasting the future and to identify the root causes of the disease.

The information extraction phase will come up with all the kinds of data in EHR, i.e., both structured and unstructured data. With the help of electronic data obtained from different types of data in bulk volumes, useful features can be extracted. Take these features as a reference and select the required features from it to maintain separate records for all the patients. Thereafter, design a predictive model for the biomedical data. This can be elaborately explained with the help of diagram, as follows.

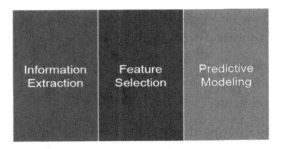

Figure 6.4 Generic Model for Big Data Analytics.

Figure 6.5 depicts the process of analyzing healthcare data using classification, regression, and patients' similarities. These prediction techniques model the huge volume of data and help to extract useful information from the resources. Let us consider a simple example in the text mining approach to analyze the data and apply that to the earlier architecture.

Example: In clinical text mining, the information extraction process is used to identify name entities from the literature. Now, feature selection will give information retrieval about the disease and symptoms. And finally, the predictive model generates a procedure for treatment.

Now observe the difference between clinical versus the biomedical texts. The biomedical text is the written medical literature, whereas the clinical text is written by clinicians in clinical settings. This difference is only with the "information extraction" phase; the remaining procedures are as usual for all kinds of medical data.

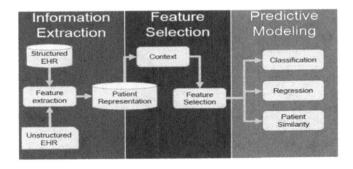

Figure 6.5 Data Analytics Procedure for Big Data.

6.3.4.1 Predictive Modeling We are using three basic prediction models for healthcare data analysis [11]:

- Regression
- Classification
- Patient similarity

Regression and classification are the basic mathematical models to analyze the data, and patient similarity is a technique to find the customized distance metric for a specific clinical context. Let us consider a case study to describe the working procedure of "patient similarity."

Case Study: On Heart Failure Onset Prediction

Let us consider the EHR database with a list of patients and their disease information [7]. From this dataset try to find the similarity between different patients under the supervision of a doctor or medical practitioner, as depicted in Figure 6.6.

In general, patient similarity, as shown in Figure 6.7, determines a customized distance metric for a specific clinical context.

After analyzing and summarizing the EHR dataset with the help of "cTAKES: clinical Text Analysis and Knowledge Extraction System," the resultant information is in the form of a similarity group, as shown in Figure 6.8.

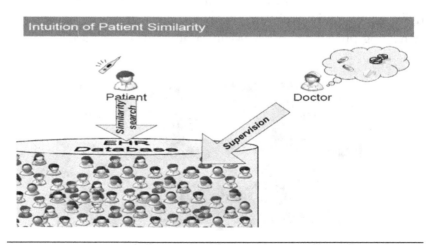

Figure 6.6 Sample Dataset with Patient's Information in the EHR.

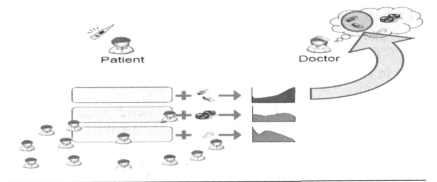

Figure 6.7 Intuition of Patient Similarity (Based on "i2b2 Informatics for Integrating Biology & the Bedside" Dataset).

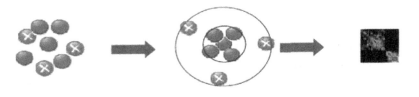

Figure 6.8 Patient Similarity Group.

Advanced data analytics on healthcare can also be performed with the help of

- Clinical prediction models
- Temporal data mining [8]
- Visual analytics
- Clinico-genomic data integration
- Information retrieval
- Privacy-preserving data publishing

For each and every technique there is acorresponding methodology in data analytics, which helps to improve the results. Now we are moving towards the challenges faced by data analytics in healthcare or biomedical health data.

6.4.1 Challenges in Clinical Text Analytics

6.4.1.1 Query Weighing The problems associated with query weighing are [7] queries are too long, not all words are useful, IDF doesn't reflect importance, and semantics will decide the weights.

6.4.1.2 Vocabulary Gaps Having problems with matching variants in words like "X Rays," "X-Ray," and "X-Rays" and matching synonyms like "CT" or "X rays." Apart from these problems we are facing one more in terms of knowledge gaps.

6.4.1.3 Pseudo-feedback To overcome the noted vocabulary gap problem, we are using a pseudo-relevance feedback technique. Here the problem is "what if a very few of the top N is relevant" and also we didn't have an idea about "which keywords to pick up."

6.4.2 Challenges in Image Data

• Extracting informative features.
• Selection of relevant features like sparse methods and dimensionality reducing techniques.
• Integration of image data with the other data variables. A few examples include:
   • Early fusion in vector-based integration.
   • Intermediate fusion in multiple kernel learning.
   • Late fusion in ensembling results from individual modalities.

6.5 Conclusion

With the immense growth of healthcare data, the data analytics and Big Data [12,13] concepts are playing a major role in the biomedical sector. To produce more accurate results on the biomedical text and EHR data, we need to do pre-processing on it and to do some analytics for better treatment and in some cases to predict the severity of the disease. In the healthcare sector, data analytics can be divided into two types. The text mining and biomedical image analysis will come under the advanced data analytics, which provides some predictive model on the sample data. The basic data analytics techniques like regression and classification will produce the commonalities between multiple diseases and help to diagnose the causes. Finally, we are going to conclude that with the help of data analytics, concepts will get good results in predicting and diagnosing different diseases with lower cost and less time.

References

1. Jane Taggart, Siaw-Teng Liaw, and Hairong Yu, Structured data quality reports to improve EHR data quality, International Journal of Medical Informatics, 2015.
2. Kasper Jensen, Knut Augestad, Rolv-Ole Lindsetmo, and Stein Skrøvseth, From unstructured EHR text to data-driven clinical decision support, International Journal of Integrated Care, 2015.
3. Alfredo Cuzzocrea, Carlo Mastroianni, and Giorgio Grasso, Private Databases On The Cloud: Models, Issues and Research Perspectives, 2016 IEEE International Conference on Big Data (Big Data), 2016.
4. B. S. Thomas, S. R. Jafarzadeh, D. K. Warren, S. McCormick, V. J. Fraser, and J. Marschall Temporal trends in the systemic inflammatory response syndrome, sepsis, and medical coding of sepsis. http://www.biomedcentral.com/1471-2253/15/169 [PMC free article] [PubMed].
5. Nils Gruschka, Vasileios Mavroeidis, Kamer Vishi, and Meiko Jensen, Privacy Issues and Data Protection in Big Data: A Case Study Analysis under GDPR, 2018 IEEE International Conference on Big Data (Big Data), 2018.
6. Healthcare Data Analytics Edited by Chandan K. Reddy, Wayne State University, Detroit, Michigan, USA. Charu C. Aggarwal, IBM T. J. Watson Research Center, Yorktown Heights, New York, USA.
7. Simon Thompson, Distributed NLP Framework to create new federated data-sets, International Journal of Population Data Science, 2018.
8. Charu C. Aggarwal and Philip S. Yu. Privacy-Preserving Data Mining: Models and Algorithms. Springer. 2008.
9. Fernando Martin-Sanchez, Guillermo Lopez-Campos, and Kathleen Gray, Biomedical Informatics Methods for Personalized Medicine and Participatory Health, Methods in Biomedical Informatics, 2014.
10. W. Raghupathi, Data Mining in Healthcare. In Healthcare Informatics: Improving Efficiency and Productivity. Edited by S. Kudyba Taylor & Francis; 2010: 211–223.
11. A. Dembosky, "Data Prescription for Better Healthcare." Financial Times, December 12, 2012, p. 19; 2012. Available from: http://www.ft.com/intl/cms/s/2/55cbca5a-4333-11e2-aa8f-00144feabdc0.html#axzz2W9cuwajK.
12. IHTT: Transforming Healthcare through Big Data Strategies for leveraging big data in the healthcare industry; 2013. http://ihealthtran.com/wordpress/2013/03/iht%C2%B2-releases-big-data-research-reportdownload-today/.
13. Healthcare Data Analytics Challenge Zhiguo Yu, Byron C. Wallace, and Todd R. Johnson, 2015 International Conference on Healthcare Informatics.
14. Emam M. Shahin, Taha E. Taha, W. Al-Nuaimy, S. El Rabaie, and Osama, Automated Detection of Diabetic Retinopathy in Blurred Digital Fundus Images, IEEE conference, 2012.

15. Komal Agicha, Priyanka Bhatia, Neha Badlani, Ashutosh Menghrajani, and Abha T ewari, Survey on Predictive Analysis of Diabetes in Young and Old Patients, IJARCSSE research paper, 5, 10, October 2015.

16. Wullianallur Raghupathi and Viju Raghupathi, Big data analytics in healthcare: promise and potential, Health Information Science and Systems 2014, 2:3, Available: http://www.hissjournal.com/content/2/1/3.

17. Healthcare Analytics and Visualization Using SEMantic Open Source Software (SEMOSS) Claire Baker, Jeannie Blackwood, Casey Hartless, Jeanne Pirro, and Abigail A. Flower University of Virginia, cjb4pf, jmb3qr, cah8ax, jdp6nc, aaf4q@virginia.edu, 978-1-5386-1848-6/17/ $31.00 ©2017 IEEE.

18. IOM (Institute of Medicine). (2009). *Health Literacy, eHealth, and Communication: Putting the Consumer First: Workshop Summary*. Washington, DC: National Academies Press. Retrieved from https://www.nap.edu/read/ 12474/chapter/2.

19. P., Lockard (2016). 5 Healthcare Marketing Trends to Watch in 2016. Retrieved March 29, 2017, from https://www.dmn3.com/dmn3-blog/5-healthcare-marketing-trends-you-should-know-about.

20. D., Gotz and D., Borland (2016, May-June). Data-driven healthcare: Challenges and opportunities for interactive visualization. *IEEE Computer Graphics and Applications*. *36*(3), 90–96. doi:10.1109/MCG. 2016.59.

7

BLUETOOTH: STATE OF THE ART, TAXONOMY, AND OPEN ISSUES FOR MANAGING SECURITY SERVICES IN HETEROGENEOUS NETWORKS

J. INDUMATHI AND J. GITANJALI

*Professor, Department of
Information Science and Technology,
Anna University, Chennai,
Tamil Nandu, India
Senior Assistant Professor, School of
Information Technology &
Engineering, VIT, Vellore,
Tamil Nadu, India*

Contents

7.1 Introduction

The digital revolution has left the modern human society with many essential and unprecedented advances; which has led to the proliferation of smart devices, with more technology usage owing to miniaturization, advances in chip design, sensors and actuators at a very low cost. Going by the European Commission estimates that by 2020 there will be between 50 and 100 billion interconnected systems this will lead to an increase in high-quality urban mobility and improvised integration of better environment and living conditions, with excellent integration and management of resources with new communication technologies. These devices need an advanced technology to communicate among themselves like the wireless communication.

   The provisioning of advanced applications and services in smart cities is possible through the ***protocols for machine to machine (M2M) communication***. The ***wireless technologies*** *like Bluetooth Low Energy (BLE) or Near-Field Communication (NFC)* have developed and matured greatly.

7.1.1 Motivation

The latest release of Bluetooth 5 comes not only with many novel features to fit itself into the disruptive technology monsters like cloud computing, artificial intelligence, robotics and Internet of Things (IoT) but has also opened up the hornet's nest of security concerns. Bluetooth SIG published the Bluetooth Core Specification Version 5.2 on January 6, 2020 . The Version 5.2 specification adds new features like *Enhanced Attribute Protocol (EATT), LE Audio, LE Isochronous Channels, and LE Power Control. EATT* is an improved version of the Attribute Protocol (ATT). *LE Audio* consumes less battery life (runs on the Bluetooth Low Energy radio), uses a new LC3 codec, permits the protocol to carry sound, and adds features like one set of headphones connecting to multiple audio sources or multiple headphones connecting to one source [*Clover, Juli 2020*]. It. BLE Audio will also add back for hearing aids [*Android Open Source Project 2020*]. Among the other most notable new features, that are worthy of mention are *data transmission up to 2 Mbps, communication up to 400 meters, and 800% in connection bandwidth.*

The increase in the data transmission bandwidth and increase in the link connection distance means that an attacker can access Bluetooth connections from even greater distances than before. The data transfer is at a fast (2 Mbps) speed, which means the attacker can get the required data before anyone realizes it.

The contributions of this chapter are

A comprehensive review to detect and categorize major security threats in Bluetooth communication so that precautionary steps can be taken.

Present an outline of Bluetooth technology with an emphasis on its security, vulnerabilities, threats, and risk mitigation solutions.

Present a quick review of the Bluetooth security gaps.

Suggest techniques to mitigate the attacks.

Suggested measures to protect the Bluetooth communication.

A bird's-eye view on the research status and future directions of Bluetooth security.

Section 1 deals with technology and the motivation for this chapter. The remainder of this chapter is organized as follows. Section 2 describes the benefits of BT technology, its use in the various applications, and real-life examples of current Bluetooth exploits. Section 3 provides an overview of the literature review, along with the issues. Section 4 explains the advantages, overview of the Bluetooth technology (core specification, connection types, classes, protocol stack of Bluetooth, security modes, BT security architecture and pairing. Section 5 presents the security architecture, features, services deployed, and its detailed design. Section 6 reviews in detail the threats and its purpose related to BT. Section 7 explains the different types of BT attack classifications based on threats, which are based on the severity of attacks and methods of penetration or post attack. Section 8 discusses the vulnerability and impact of approaches to escalate the range of Bluetooth and its categories (configuration vulnerability, design vulnerability, implementation vulnerability). Section 9 describes the risk mitigation techniques. Section 10 explains the countermeasures (*security checklist with guiding principle and suggestions*) that should be applied to overcome the attacks, threats, and vulnerabilities of BT. Section 11 concludes the chapter with an outline of BT.

7.2 Rationale Behind The Study

7.2.1 Efficacy of Bluetooth

Bluetooth is used for *low bandwidth applications* like wireless networking between PCs, dial-up Internet access on personal computers or PDAs, real-time location systems (RTLS). Bluetooth devices can be used to predict (for instance, travel times and road congestion for motorists) and for safeguarding personal information from mobile phones. Mobile telephony, mice, portable printers, PC, organizers, audio helmets, assistive technologies, Hi-Fi systems, numerical cameras, remote banking payment, and car applications are a few applications of Bluetooth technology. The Bluetooth Smart Mesh technology is overriding the new markets as automotive, smart building, smart city, and smart home and industry automation. Bluetooth is used for smart keys, for sensitive encryption and authentication, and also just for connecting any medical devices to wireless infrastructure [1,2].

Bluetooth is implemented for several different use cases such as indoor proximity systems [3], micro location [3], earthquake monitoring systems [4,5], and vehicle communication with mobile phones [6].

A few of the **key benefits** of Bluetooth technology are *replacement of cables with wireless, ease of file sharing* (devices form a piconet to support file sharing), *Internet connectivity* (share that access with other Bluetooth devices), and *wireless synchronization* (provides automatic synchronization between Bluetooth-enabled devices). However, these suffer from **issues** like *easier eavesdropping, easier to disrupt, and jam wireless RF communication*, and hence good countermeasures are needed to protect against new threats, vulnerabilities and attacks.

7.2.2 Approaches for Bluetooth Range Escalation

The real time *LE-enabled project leaves the researchers in a Catch-22 when it is unable to cover adequate range.* The conundrum faced by the engineers can be flattened by four ways to extend the range of Bluetooth-enabled products. ***The crucial point is to pick the secure approach.*** The four approaches that are needed to outspread the range are:

- Using the long-range feature (coded PHY) in Bluetooth 5
- Amplifying the signal
- Employing a repeater to relay the signal
- Utilizing LE

i. **Using the Long-Range Feature in Bluetooth 5** – LE Long Range/Coded PHY is a special capability of Bluetooth 5, which permits enlarged range by increasing the output power and by using bit expansion using Forward Error Correction (FEC) coding. It directs each bit in the data packet as coded 2- or 8-bits so as to offer more devices to receive transmissions at farer distances. Repetition increases the range.

ii. **Amplifying the Signal** – This second approach increases the signal strength by increasing the power being channeled into the antenna to produce a stronger RF output. This "brute-force" method has some caveats like the limits fixed by the certification standards on how much power amplification can be exploited. Amplifying the signal consumes uses more battery than operating a device.

iii. **Employing a Repeater to Relay the Signal** – A repeater device serves as a go-between that can enlarge the distance between two Bluetooth devices that is essential to communicate – repeating the message until it is received by the target device. This approach works fine in a more static environment when the physical layout of devices and repeaters do not change over time and when the RF landscape is static. But in a more dynamic environment, this approach can drift over time. In a relatively static environment, repeating the signal has a number of advantages but comes with many caveats.

iv.   **Utilizing LE** – In a LE network, messages are spread across the network of interconnected devices until it reaches the intended recipients, via the LE devices themselves. LE deployments should exploit the Low Power Node feature (maximizes lifetime in sleep mode) in the mesh protocol, and the "Friend" mode (accountable for the active listening role that captures incoming messages, and checks with the friend for applicable messages only seldomly) for nearby devices in the network to conserve battery power. The possession of Coded PHY and LE can be both leveraged in a single implementation. There is a possibility of deployment of a hybrid proprietary solution where the mesh adverts are sent as Coded PHY messages. The cons to this approach are that networks exploiting a proprietary setup like this have interoperability problems with normal mesh deployments, but there are scenarios where it is preferred for the strong security of mesh.

7.2.3 Security System is Fractional

The vulnerability arising from the Bluetooth is quite alarming and it does not serve the purpose for which it is designed. There are many applications like home automation products from cloud cameras like Google's Nest Cam to Bluetooth-enabled pressure cookers. Say, for example, the vulnerability in the security cameras are quite alarming. Dropcam, Dropcam Pro, Nest Cam Outdoor, and Nest Cam Indoor running version 5.2.1 of Nest's firmware can be wirelessly attacked via Bluetooth to clatter and sojourn recording footage. There are **three vulnerabilities are in camera firmware version 5.2.1, and no solution is publicly available**

1. An attacker can trigger a buffer overflow in the camera by pinging it an overlong Wi-Fi SSID parameter via Bluetooth Low Energy (BLE). This triggers a buffer overflow condition, which causes the cameras to stop recording, crash and reboot.

2. The miscreant sends a long Wi-Fi password parameter to the camera. This triggers a buffer overflow condition, which causes the cameras to stop recording, crash and reboot.

3. It bashes the camera from its linked Wi-Fi network entirely. Attackers can blast the camera with a new SSID connect to, which blows it off its network; as it is linking the new SSID, which apparently doesn't exist, it rejoins the previous wireless network about 90 seconds later. From then on, the device stops recording footage to its cloud-connected backend.

Bluetooth is enabled by default in the cameras and stays on at all times so the gadgets can be reconfigured over the air. This leaves them vulnerable to attack.

To get an in-depth knowledge of the challenges, let us skim a short literature review.

7.3 Literature Survey

As Bluetooth technology continues to evolve and improve, security experts continue their research with the goal of obtaining information on the newest version of the technology to gain insight, enhance security, and develop updated versions. **Security in Bluetooth networks** depends on (i) security of the Bluetooth medium, (ii) the security of Bluetooth protocols, and (iii) the security parameters used in Bluetooth communication.

R. Bouhenguel et al. [7] points out three methods designed into Bluetooth protocol to provide security: (i) Use of pseudo-random frequency hopping, (ii) Restricted authentication, and (iii) Encryption [7]. The generic Bluetooth protocol includes three security modes: (a) non-secure, (b) service-level security, and (c) link-level security.

In the setting of the prevailing security problems, many research works have been done, and all the activities are mostly focused on providing a competent, brief, and effective pairing mechanism between Bluetooth devices. Some exemplary research work has been cited in Monson, Heidi [8], and Mana Feham and Bensaber [9].

  Nateq Be-Nazir Ibn and Tarique [10] presented the threats present in Bluetooth from 2007. Panse and Panse [11] explained the Bluetooth vulnerabilities. Hassan Bibon Hossain and Atiquzzzaman [12] gives an overview of Bluetooth technology, its background and architecture, different types of attacks, and prevention methods. Darroudi and Gomez [13] gave an overview of BLE Mesh Networks and briefly touched on security in IoT networks. Zafari and Papapanagiotou [4] explains the information on wireless security and physical layer-based attacks.

7.3.1 Challenges/Issues

- The **Bluetooth devices possess an inherent** big security risk due to the very short, regularly only four-digit, fixed PIN codes.
- There is a lacuna from the user's perspective, as they do not have any clear idea on how to configure their Bluetooth devices' security settings correctly to safeguard the sensitive data.
- As there is no strong encryption mechanism in by default in many kinds of Bluetooth devices, it is susceptible to attacks like reflection attacks and interception of packets attacks.
- Bluetooth built-in security should be used in combination with an extra safety facility.
- Compulsory security is needed at the application level to overcome the security issues.
- Application layer key exchange and encryption methods are to be used to provide extra security in addition to the Bluetooth built-in security.
- The factory settings of Bluetooth factory must ensure the encryption by default, as many users do not know about its presence or do not know how to set it up effectively. The second solution is to mandatorily set Bluetooth encryption, which requires minor changes to the Bluetooth specification.
- SWEYNTOOTH [Garbelini, M. E., Chattopadhyay, S., & Wang, C.] apprehends a family of 12 vulnerabilities across diverse BLE software development kits (SDKs) of seven major

system-on-a-chip (SoC) vendors. The vulnerabilities depict flaws precisely for BLE SoC implementations that permit an attacker in radio range to activate deadlocks, crashes, and buffer overflows or totally bypass security reliant on the conditions.

- Zhiqiang Lin [14,15] points out the intrinsic design flaw that makes BT devices and the mobile apps that work with them vulnerable to hacking. **Flaws (leads to vulnerability) noted in the BT devices are:** (i) When Bluetooth low energy devices (like a fitness tracker, smart thermostat, smart speaker, or smart home assistant) is primarily paired to a mobile app, it broadcasts a UUID – a universally unique identifier – to permit the corresponding apps on the phone to identify the Bluetooth device, creating a link that allows the phone and device to talk to one another. The UUID is embedded into the mobile app code and it makes the devices vulnerable to a fingerprinting attack. (ii) When Bluetooth low energy devices are operating.

- Issues arising when the Bluetooth aims to link diverse IoT devices over a long-range, low-bandwidth network.

- The process of BT can be broken down. The McAfee Researchers reported Bluetooth Low Energy misconfiguration issues in a smart padlock known as BoxLock. The device is designed to work in "Just Works Mode" by using a Bluetooth Low Energy configuration that aids the devices to pair without any passwords or other cryptographic protections, which could connect to any lock, analyze the device's BLE commands (read-write mode), and discern which one gave the unlock order. BoxLock ran into two Bluetooth issues. It deployed a relatively insecure version of it for a device to use and left the Bluetooth traffic out in the open for hackers. Researchers highlight the Bluetooth security risks arising from the growth of Bluetooth spreads. The hackers attack via the consumer settings, like smart home devices and wearables – almost everything.

- Bluetooth has to compete with its own brand reputation.

- Bluetooth privacy concerns are still in their infancy and need to be solved.

7.3.2 Research Works and Gaps

The **research works and gaps discussed can be classified** as follows:

- The usage of DES and RSA for Bluetooth communication offers integrity and confidentiality, with the limitation that these protocols are too lengthy and will surge the communication delay.
- The one user shared secret key which is used for pairing mechanism is not secure and hence use the concept of two shared secret parameters.
- As the majority of vulnerabilities occur, it is easy to crack the Bluetooth address of devices. So, therefore use an alias of Bluetooth address for Bluetooth communication.
- Markus Jakobsson and Susanne Vitzel (2008) project the different ways of generating link keys and initialization keys keeping major vulnerabilities in mind.
- Jun-Zhao, Douglas Howie, and Antti and Jaakko Sauvol proposed several link key management, authentication and encryption schemes to make Bluetooth more secure and robust and proposed many countermeasures to handle security issues.
- In 2010 Wuling et al. proposed that the present encryption and authentication algorithm are susceptible to MITM and pin cracking attacks. He recommended a hybrid system of DES and RSA. Since DES is symmetric and RSA is asymmetric, both together can provide confidentiality and integrity.
- **Using the Long-Range Feature in Bluetooth 5** – When using LE Long Range/Coded PHY, there is a trade-off in terms of speed of transmissions and throughput of data transfer, which is still a challenge.
- **Amplifying the Signal** – The signal amplification in exchange for less battery life decreases the energy efficiency, which is still a challenge.
- **Employing a Repeater to Relay the Signal** – Commissioning is more complex and insecure in deployments that exploit repeaters. In order to maintain secure communications through this approach, all of the devices in the network must be provided with security protocols that have levels of trust with the

repeater device. This becomes a nightmare not only while commissioning but also when the repeating device ever fails and needs to be replaced. Every time the devices in the network have to be re-commissioned in order to have a secure connection with the new repeating device, this can cause a problem.

• **Utilizing LE** – The cons to this approach are that networks exploiting a proprietary setup like this have interoperability problems with normal mesh deployments

7.4 Overview of Bluetooth Technology

The Bluetooth devices work in the ranges from 10 and 100 m. A directional antenna and an amplifier can be used to extend the range of Bluetooth over a mile away. The Bluetooth technical specification are shown in Table 7.1.

According to the Bluetooth Core Specification Version 5.2 | Vol 1, Part A, document, there are **two forms of Bluetooth wireless technology systems,** namely, **Basic Rate (BR) and Low Energy (LE).** Both the BR and LE systems (Table 7.2) are used to discover devices and establish connection and connection mechanisms.

The Bluetooth Core Specification Version 5.2 says the **BR system** comprises Enhanced Data Rate (EDR) Alternate Media Access Control (MAC), and Physical (PHY) layer extensions. BR system offers synchronous and asynchronous connections with data rates of

Table 7.1 Bluetooth Technical Specification

CONNECTION	SPREAD SPECTRUM FREQUENCY
Aggregate data rate	0.721-1 Mbps
Data security	128 bit key
Data security and encryption	8-128 bits configurable
Frequency band	2.4 Ghz ISM
Mac scheduling scheme	FH-CDMA
Modulation technique	Gaussian frequency shift
Range	10-100 m
Supported stations	8 stations (per piconet)
Transmission power	>20 dbm
Voice channels	3

Table 7.2   Key Differences Between Bluetooth BR/EDR and LE

CHARACTERISTIC	BLUETOOTH BR/EDR	BLUETOOTH LE
Device Address Privacy	None	Private device addressing available
Discovery/Connect	Inquiry/Paging	Advertising
Encryption Algorithm	E0/SAFER +	AES-CCM
Max Data Rate	1–3 Mbps	1 Mbps via GFSK modulation
Max Output Power	100 mW (20 dBm)	10 mW (10 dBm)
Number of Piconet Slaves	7 (active)/255 (total)	Unlimited
RF Physical Channels	79 channels with 1 MHz channel spacing	40 channels with 2 MHz channel spacing
Typical Range	30 meters	50 meters

721.2 kb/s for Basic Rate, 2.1 Mb/s for EDR and high-speed operation up to 54 Mb/s with the 802.11 AMP.

The Bluetooth Core Specification Version 5.2 further says that the **LE system** includes features premeditated to permit products that necessitate lower current consumption, lower complexity, and lower cost than BR/EDR. The LE system is used for use cases and applications with lower data rates and has lower duty cycles. The LE system includes an optional 2 Mb/s physical layer data rate and also offers isochronous data transfer in a connection-oriented and connectionless mechanism that uses the isochronous transports. Depending on the use case or application, one system including any optional parts may be more optimal than the other.

Bluetooth Connection types define the ways Bluetooth devices can exchange data. Bluetooth has three connection types to exchange data, viz., **Asynchronous Connection-Less, Synchronous Connection-Oriented and Extended SCO.**

The Bluetooth protocol stack is made up of the following:

Radio (RF) layer – This layer modulates/demodulates the data into RF signals. It outlines the physical characteristics of Bluetooth transceiver. It expresses two types of physical links: connection-less and connection-oriented.

Baseband Link layer – This layer establishes the connection within a piconet.

Link Manager protocol layer – This layer manages the previously established links and performs the authentication and encryption processes.

Logical Link Control and Adaption protocol layer/the heart of the Bluetooth protocol stack – This layer permits the communication amid upper and lower layers of the Bluetooth protocol stack. The data packets received from upper layers are packaged and sent to the lower layers in the desirable format. It also does segmentation and multiplexing.

SDP layer (Service Discovery Protocol) – The SDP layer permits the device to realize the services accessible on another Bluetooth-enabled device.

RF comm layer (Radio Frontend Component) – This layer offers serial interface with WAP and OBEX.

OBEX (Object Exchange) – OBEX is a communication protocol to exchange objects among two devices.

WAP (Wireless Access Protocol) – WAP is useful for Internet access.

TCS (Telephony Control Protocol) – TCP offers telephony service.

Application layer – This layer facilitates the interaction of the user with the application.

Bluetooth, a wireless technology standard and an open specification for short-range wireless communication and networking, was developed by Ericsson and is maintained by the Special Lobby Special Interest Group (SIG) of Bluetooth and is accessorily standardized by the IEEE under the reference IEEE 802.15.1.

The Bluetooth specification splits Bluetooth devices into three classes (Table 7.3):

Most Bluetooth devices are Class 2 or Class 3.

Table 7.3 Bluetooth Classes

CLASS	POWER (DBM)	POWER (MW)	DISTANCE (M)	SAMPLE DEVICES
Class 1	20	100	~ 100	BT Access Point, dongles
Class 2	4	2.5	~ 10	Keyboards, mice
Class 3	0	1	~ 1	Mobile phone headset

Bluetooth protocols – The Bluetooth stack is designed and developed to permit use of Bluetooth by a variety of communication applications. Normally, an application will only use one vertical slice of this stack.

The Bluetooth protocols layer and their linked protocols are enumerated here:

- **Adopted Protocols:** IrMC, OBEX, PPP, UDP/TCP/IP, vCal, vCard, WAE,WAP
- **Applicative protocols:** PPP, TCP/IP, OBEX, WAP, vCard, VCal, WAE
- **Bluetooth Core Protocols Baseband:** L2CAP, LMP, SDP
- **Interfacing protocols/Cable Replacement Protocol:** RFCOMM
- **Telephony Control Protocol/Applicative control specifications:** AT-commands, TCS Binary
- **Lower layer protocols:** Baseband, L2CAP, LMP, service discovery protocol (SDP)

The **host controller interface (HCI)** in the Bluetooth specification also defines a command interface to the baseband controller, link manager, and entry to hardware status and control registers. Bluetooth devices use **four types of addresses**, namely, BD ADDR, LT ADDR, PM ADDR, and AR ADDR.

7.5 Bluetooth Security Architecture

7.5.1 Bluetooth Security Features

The example shown in Table 7.4 depicts the Bluetooth security offered between the phone and the laptop, although IEEE 802.11 security guards the WLAN link between the laptop and the IEEE 802.11 access point (AP). Communications on the wired network are unprotected by Bluetooth or IEEE 802.11 security competences. In order to provide an end-to-end security usage of higher-layer security solutions atop the security features should be included in Bluetooth and IEEE 802.11. The Bluetooth Core security architecture possess several security mechanisms.

Table 7.4 Security Features of Bluetooth Core Security Architecture

SECURITY FEATURES	UTILIZES/BASED ON
BR/EDR Legacy Pairing	E21 or E22 algorithms based on SAFER +
Device authentication	E1 algorithm, based on SAFER +.
Encryption	E0 algorithm derived from the Massey-Rueppel algorithm
Message integrity	no provision for cryptographic. Though CRC can offer integrity protection, it is not considered to offer cryptographic integrity as it can be easily counterfeited
Secure Simple Pairing	FIPS-approved algorithms (SHA-256, HMAC-SHA-256 and the P-192 elliptic curve) and four association models: Just Works, Numeric Comparison, Passkey Entry and Out-Of-Band
LE Legacy Pairing	AES-CCM encryption and four association models: Just Works, Numeric Comparison, Passkey Entry and Out-Of-Band. It also offers signed data and a privacy feature.
Secure Connections on the BR/EDR physical transport promotes Secure Simple Pairing	P-256 elliptic curve and device authentication to use FIPS-approved algorithms (HMAC-SHA-256 and AES-CTR). Secure Connections also enhances message integrity (AES-CCM).
Secure Connections on the LE physical transport upgrades LE Legacy Pairing	FIPS-approved algorithms (AES-CMAC and P-256 elliptic curve) and acclimatizes the Numeric Comparison association model of Secure Simple Pairing to be used on the Bluetooth LE physical transport. It also embraces provisions for a key created using Secure Connections on whichever physical transport to preclude the need for the user to pair a second time on the other physical transport.

7.5.2 Security Services

The Bluetooth security model consists of five discrete security features, namely, the bonding, device authentication, encryption, message integrity and pairing.

- **Authentication** – It is used to verify the identity of the devices that are communicating. But user authentication is not offered natively.

- **Authorization** – It ensures that the device is approved to use a service and permits the control of resources.
- **Confidentiality** – It guarantees only the authorized devices to access and analyze data and averts information negotiation caused by eavesdropping.
- **Message Integrity** – It ensures that the message transferred between the two Bluetooth devices is intact without any alteration.
- **Pairing/Bonding** – It ensures that one or more shared secret keys are generated and stored

Note that Bluetooth does not provide security services like audit and non-repudiation.

7.5.3 Bluetooth Security Modes

The BT versions (up to 2.1) outlines four different security modes that a device can implement. In Bluetooth technology, a device can be in only one of the subsequent security modes at a time:

Security Mode 1 (Nonsecure) – A non-secure mode. Authentication and encryption are sidestepped leaving this mode deprived of all security measures. Mode 1 is simply supported in BT 2.0 + EDR and earlier versions [16].

Security Mode 2 (Service-level Enforced) – This is a service-level enforced security mode and is supported by all Bluetooth devices. Based on the notion of authorization, decision is taken as to grant access to specific devices or people, and this is controlled by the centralized security manager. Once when the physical link is established, security measures take place

Security Mode 3 (Link-level Enforced) – This mode commands authentication and encryption for all links to and from the device. The physical link is established, even before the security measures take place. Security Mode 3 is only supported in Bluetooth 2.0 + EDR and earlier devices [16].

Security Mode 4 (Service-level Enforced) – This mode is enforced on the service level, after the establishment of physical link. The pairing mechanism uses Elliptic Curve Diffie Hellman

(ECDH) techniques. Services sustained by Mode 4 must be classified as one of the following:

- Authenticated Link Key required.
- Unauthenticated Link Key required.
- No security required.

This is obligatory for communication among devices in compliance to Bluetooth 2.1 + EDR or newer versions [16].

7.5.4 Bluetooth Service Levels

Security requirements for services protected by Security Mode 4 is classified as one of the following:

- Level 4: Authenticated link key using Secure Connections required
- Level 3: Authenticated link key required
- Level 2: Unauthenticated link key required
- Level 1: No security required
- Level 0: No security required (only allowed for SDP)

These five levels (SL 0, 1, 2, 3, and 4) address diverse protective technologies against cybersecurity threats, which consist of:

- Man-in-the-Middle (MitM) threats
- DDoS attacks
- User interaction
- Encryption strength

SL 0 hosts no cybersecurity protections of any kind and is vulnerable to plainly every likely attack all the way to SL 4, which hosts all of the items noted earlier. These SLs are characterized in such a way to permit elasticity for implementers dependent on their requirements, particularly when using Secure Simple Pairing (SSP).

The SP 800 121 document outlines a series of important security features and risk mitigation strategies. **The key highlights** include the following:

- **Link Keys:** A secure authentication is the creation of a secret symmetric key (called as link key or long-term key) for Bluetooth applications. The NIST document specifies how the creation is done in various versions. For ***Personal Identification Number (PIN)/legacy pairing,*** the link key is created when the user enters a PIN, while in ***low energy devices***, the key is created by each device and is at no time is distributed.

- **Authentication:** Bluetooth devices validate to prove their identity or for verification (claimant/verifier scheme) in a challenge-response style. The legacy devices are authenticated via a PIN/legacy pairing, while in innovative applications (like secure automotive applications), this occurs using a secure authentication using SSP and the P-256 Elliptic Curve.
- **Encryption:** The NIST mentions that the AES-CMAC and P-256 elliptic curve provides the utmost secure combination for high-security requirements (needed in the highest SL 4). Additionally, implementers will need to guarantee that only FIPS-approved algorithms are used, especially for BLE specifications. s
- **Vulnerabilities:** The NIST outlines several vulnerabilities like eavesdropping and attacks on the link keys, reusing the same keys and insecure storage of said keys, spoofing insecure devices to obtain keys from other devices they pair with, short PINs without the use of random number generators, sharing the key from a master device to other piconets, and usage of weak encryption algorithms, among others and some countermeasures.

Users characterize the first layer of security in Bluetooth technology. It provides a very flexible security framework, which commands when to involve a user (e.g. to provide a PIN) and what actions the basic fundamental BT protocol layers follow to support the desired security check-ups

1. Store security-related information on services and devices
2. Answer access needs by protocol implementations or applications
3. Impose authentication and/or encryption before linking to the application.
4. Initiate or process input from the device user to set up trusted relations on device level.
5. Initiate pairing and query PIN entry by the user. PIN entry might also be finished by an application.

Table 7.5   Secure Simple Pairing and the Secure Connection Feature of the Devices

SECURE NATURE OF DEVICES	SECURE SIMPLE PAIRING HAS APPROXIMATELY...
Devices with no feature of Secure Connections	96 bits of entropy using the FIPS approved P-192 elliptic curve
Devices with Secure Connections feature	128 bits of entropy using the FIPS-approved P-256 elliptic curve

7.5.5 Security Features of Bluetooth BR/EDR

Bluetooth BR/EDR outlines authentication and encryption security procedures that can be obligatory during diverse stages of communication setup amid peer devices. **Link-level enforced** refers to authentication and encryption setup procedures which occur prior to establishment of Bluetooth physical link. **Service-level enforced** refers to authentication and encryption setup procedures which occur post establishment of Bluetooth physical link and logical channels partially established.

7.5.5.1 BR/EDR Secure Simple Pairing

7.5.5.1.1 Security goals offered   Security goals offered are the protection against passive eavesdropping and man-in-the-middle (MITM) attacks (active eavesdropping). It offers a maximum-security level by using a 16 character, alphanumeric, case-sensitive PIN with BR/EDR legacy pairing that often uses a 4-digit PIN or a fixed PIN of recurrently known values deliberately limiting the security on the link.

- **Passive eavesdropping protection** – Secure Simple Pairing uses Elliptic Curve Diffie Hellman (ECDH) public key cryptography. ECDH offers a very high degree of forte to counter the passive eavesdropping attacks but it may be susceptible to MITM attacks.
- **Man-in-the-middle protection** – Secure Simple Pairing suggests two user aided numeric methods, namely, the numerical comparison or passkey entry, by using a six-digit number. Secure Simple Pairing defends the user from MITM attacks, because it offers 1 in 1000000 chance that a MITM could

mount a positive attack. This level is selected because the users can be alerted to the latent presence of a MITM attacker when the linking process fails as a consequence of an unsuccessful MITM attack.

The security key hierarchy is varied and depends on if a physical link is using Secure Connections or legacy security procedures and algorithms.

7.5.5.1.2 Association models Secure Simple Pairing uses four association models stated as Just Works, Numeric Comparison, Out of Band, and Passkey Entry.

- **Just Works – Just Works are used in scenarios** where both devices do not have the provision for displaying a six-digit number or have a keyboard to enter the six decimal digits. Just Works offers protection against passive eavesdropping.
- **Numeric Comparison** – There are two uses for numeric comparison, namely (i) it ensures the user that the correct devices are linked with each other (preferred when the device does not have a unique number) and (ii) protects against MITM attacks.
- **Out of Band (OOB)** – The Out of Band mechanism is used to both discover the devices as well as to exchange or transfer cryptographic numbers used in the pairing process. **OOB offers protection against** MITM attacks
- **Passkey Entry – Passkey Entry is used in scenarios where** one device has input capability and the other device has output capabilities to display six digits.

7.5.5.2 Secure Connections-only Mode Only FIPS-approved algorithms are used on the BR/EDR physical transport, on the BR/EDR physical transport in this mode. This mode is preferred when high device security is needed. The host will impose that the P-256 elliptic curve is used all through pairing, the secure authentication sequences are used, and AES-CCM is used for encryption.

Only FIPS-approved algorithms are used on the LE physical transport in this mode. This mode is preferred when high device security is needed. The host will impose that the P-256 elliptic curve is used all through pairing.

In case a BR/EDR/LE device is constituted in Secure Connections Only Mode, then the BR/EDR and the LE transports will be in Secure Connection Only Mode.

7.5.5.3 LE Security   The 5.2 version of the Core Specification enhances a new LE security mode that permits transmission and reception of encrypted isochronous data over the Broadcast Isochronous Stream (BIS) logical transport.

LE Legacy Pairing association models are similar to BR/EDR Secure Simple Pairing from the user viewpoint but have alterations in the quality of the safety provided.

7.5.5.3.1 Association models   Bluetooth LE uses association models stated as Just Works, Out of Band, and Passkey Entry. LE legacy pairing does not possess an equivalent for Numeric Comparison.

- **Just Works – Just Works are used in scenarios** where both devices do not have the provision for displaying a six-digit number or have a keyboard to enter the six decimal digits. Just Works offers protection against passive eavesdropping.
- **Out of Band (OOB)** – The Out of Band mechanism is used to both discover the devices as well as to exchange or transfer cryptographic numbers used in the pairing process. **OOB offers protection against** MITM attacks
- **Passkey Entry – Passkey Entry is used in scenarios where** one device has input capability and the other device has output capabilities to display six digits.

In LE legacy pairing, Just Works and Passkey Entry do not offer passive eavesdropping protection, as the Secure Simple Pairing uses Elliptic Curve Diffie – Hellman, whereas LE legacy pairing does not. The use of each association model is grounded on the I/O capabilities of the devices.

7.5.5.3.2 Key generation   The key is created by the host on each LE device. Each one of the keys among the multiple keys has a specific purpose, like **Confidentiality, Authentication, and Device**

Identity. In LE, the key utilized to offer confidentiality and authentication is created by coalescing contributions from each device during pairing.

7.5.5.3.3 Encryption AES-CCM cryptography is used for encryption in Bluetooth LE. Encryption is achieved in the controller.

Signed Data Bluetooth LE has the capability to transmit authenticated data over an unencrypted ATT carrier amid two devices with a reliable connection. The data is signed by a Connection Signature Resolving Key (CSRK), and the signature is appended after the Data PDU by the transmitting device. The receiving device confirms the signature and if the signature is proved the Data PDU is presumed to originate from the trusted source. The signature is made up of a Message Authentication Code created by the signing algorithm and a counter. The counter is used to guard against a replay attack and is increased on each signed Data PDU sent.

7.5.5.3.4 Privacy Feature The Bluetooth device address keeps recurrently changing, and this diminishes the facility to track a Bluetooth LE device.

Variants of the privacy features are (i) private addresses are determined and created by the host. (ii) Private addresses are determined and created by the controller without relating the host subsequently the host offers the controller device identity information. This encompasses the host when the resolving list in the controller cannot store all the device identity resolving keys essential for bonded devices.

Modes of Privacy

1. **Device privacy mode** – The device is aware of the privacy of the device and will receive advertising packets from peer devices that hold their identity address and a private address, even if the peer device has dispersed its IRK in the past.
2. **Network privacy mode** – The device will only receive advertising packets from peer devices that hold private addresses. By default, network privacy mode is used when private addresses are determined and created by the controller.

The host upholds a resolving list by joining and eliminating device identities. The host may offer the controller with a whole resolving list or a subset of the resolving list. A device identity entails the peer's identity address and a local and peer's IRK pair.

The controller performs address resolution and the host needs to state to a peer device that is involved in the resolving list, it uses the peer's device identity address.

Incoming events from the controller to the host use the peer's device identity, on condition that the peer's device address has been resolved. If the controller cannot resolve the peer's device identity address in an advertisement, it may pass the event to the host for resolution in the host.

Device filtering is made possible when address resolution is achieved in the controller since the peer's device identity address can be resolved preceding to inspecting if it is in the white list.

When address resolution is completed in the host, the device uses more power and the device filtering must be inactivated.

Bluetooth offers four distinct connectivity and discoverability modes, which can be selected by the user of a Bluetooth device:

---

i.   **Silent** – Device monitors the Bluetooth traffic and does not accept any connections.

i.   **Private (non-discoverable)** – Device cannot be discovered and it doesn't admit any connections if their address is known to the master.

i.   **Public (discoverable)** – Device can be discovered and will accept connections from prospective masters.

i.   **LE (Low-Energy) Privacy** – Device can deliver messages to other Bluetooth devices in connectionless mode.

The security level linked to each of these modes depends on the pairing operation. When two devices initiate a connection, a shared key is created and secured through a set of protocols or a single protocol designed to surge the security level of the process.

7.6 Threats in Bluetooth

Threat taxonomy is designed to create a point of reference for threats met, while providing a possibility to shuffle, arrange, amend, and detail threat definitions. Attempts to profile and classify the attackers have been done by R. Brooks et al. [17] and M. Wolf et al. (2005)], where models of attack scenarios have been defined. We reproduce in Figure 7.2 the model proposed by [17], derived from the attack taxonomy used by the CERT [18–20] and adapted to an automotive context. Moreover, in order to gain more knowledge about the attackers, Verendel et al. [21,22] considered the deployment of honeypots in in-vehicle networks, gathering attack data as the attackers have been done in [17] and where models of attack scenarios have been defined.

7.7 Bluetooth Attack Classification

A comprehensible threat taxonomy is needed for all the security stakeholders, ranging from security experts to novice users of security. The Bluetooth comprehensible taxonomy is needed for its design, development, and implementation.

7.7.1 Attack Classification Based on Threats

- **Denial Of Service** – Battery exhaustion, signal jamming, BlueSYN, Blueper, BlueJacking, vCard Blaster – *Medium*: Main purpose is to deny resources to a target by saturating the communication channel.
- **Fuzzer** – BluePass, Bluetooth Stack Smasher, BlueSmack, Tanya, BlueStab-*Medium*: Main purpose is to submit non-standard input to get different results.
- **Malware** – BlueBag, Caribe, CommWarrior - *Medium*: Main purpose is to carry out attacks typically using self-replicating form of software.
- **Man In The Middle** – BT-SSP-Printer-MITM, BlueSpooof, bthidproxy –*High*: Main purpose is to place a device between

two connected devices. All the information sent through the channel are available to the device in between.

- **Obfuscation** – Bdaddr, hciconfig, Spooftooph – *Low*: Main purpose is to hide the attacker's identity.
- **Range Extension** – BlueSniping, bluetooone, Vera-NG – *Low*: Main purpose is to extend the device range so that attacks could be conducted from far way distance
- **Sniffing** – FTS4BT, Merlin, BlueSniff, HCIDump, Wireshark, kismet –*Medium*: Main purpose is to capture the Bluetooth traffic in transit.
- **Surveillance** – Blueprinting, bt_audit, redfang, War-nibbling, Bluefish, dptool, Bluescanner, BTScanner-*Low*: Main purpose is to observe and gather information about the device and its location
- **Unauthorized Direct Data Access** – Bloover, BlueBug, BlueSnarf, BlueSnarf++, BTCrack, Car Whisperer, HeloMoto, btpincrack – *High*: Main purpose is to gather private information in an unauthorized manner. This is very serious as very important information can be stolen.

7.7.2 Attack Classification Based on Severity of Attacks

Bluetooth attacks are classified based on methods of penetration or post-attack effects on the target. Based on the extent of post effects on the target, the severity of attacks is classified as high, medium, and low.

- *High severity attacks* gain full control of the target to steal, alter, or delete data from the memory or external storage and can cause financial damage. *Examples* – Backdoor Attack, Blue-Bugging, Blue-Snarfing, Car Whisperer, Free Calling, Off-Line PIN Recovery, PIN Cracking Attack.
- *Medium severity attacks* steal data and extract information from the target during the data transmission. *Examples* – Blue-Bump, Brute-Force Attack, Forced Re-pairing Attack, MAC Address Spoofing Attack, Man-in-the Middle Attack, Relay Attack
- In the *low severity attacks*, the target activities of the target are monitored without any disturbance. *Examples* – Blue-Chop,

Blue-Jacking, Blue-Printing, Blue-Stumbling, Blue-Tracking, DoS Attacks

7.7.3 Attack Classification Based on Impact

(1) Pin Theft Attack – The PIN is stolen to establish connection with the target device to carry out malicious activities. The attacker snoops the pairing process, gets the necessary data, and uses a brute-force algorithm to find the used PIN. Next, the attacker lists all the probable variations of the PIN. To identify the correct initialization key, they use a 128-bit random number, if the MAC address of Bluetooth device is already known. The collected data is used to find the shared session link. The PIN is easily cracked if all the collected information is correct PIN can be easily cracked [[23]; D. K. Nilsson et al. [24]].

Pin cracking attack: [*Going Around with Bluetooth in Full Safety*] The shared secret user-defined PIN number is cracked by the dictionary attack or a simple PIN-guessing attack to snap the Bluetooth communication link keys.

(1.1) Off-Line PIN Recovery Attack – An off-line PIN recovery attack is the method of seizing the PIN in order to get entrance to the target device. By means of a device MAC Address (48 bits) and the PIN code with its length, an initialization key [IK (128 bits)] is created. This initialization key is used by the devices to create two random values, namely, RAND-1 (128 bits) and RAND-2 (128 bits). The devices utilize the two random values to produce the link key in order to launch connection. To calculate the PIN, a decryption algorithm is used. Discovery of the correct PIN is possible if the PIN is short in length [23,25]. Upon recovery of the PIN, the attacker pairs with the target device and can snip data deprived of the permission of the target.

(1.2) Eavesdropping Attack – The attacker knocks into the communication between the two target devices and snips information. The following subsection elucidates two of the eavesdropping attacks.

(1.2.1) Man-in-the-Middle Attack – The attacker coaxes both the target devices to use the same hopping sequence, so that the attacker can effortlessly breach the transmission security [26]. The attacker captures the transmitted data between the two devices in such a way that the targets believe nothing is wrong, but it is the method of accessing and modifying the data that is communicated between the Bluetooth devices by using a bogus Access Point device. In [27,28], the authors mentioned that a Man-in-the-Middle attack may also occur due to flaws in the pairing process, when a device wants to link to a device but erroneously connects to a different device.

(1.2.2) Relay Attack or Reflection attacks – The sender and the receiver devices are both targeted and connected to two dummy devices without their knowledge. Both the targets communicate with each other, and the attacker device continuously eavesdrops on their communication [24] and manipulates it as desired. This attack is not noticed.

(1.3) Target Device Cloning Attack – By robbing the device address of the target, the attacker clones herself as that of the target and follows the attack.

(1.3.1) MAC Address Spoofing Attack – This attack is designed to rob the data from the targeted device. The MAC addresses of two Bluetooth devices can be spotted by snooping the communications. The attacker gets the data and then he may forward the data to the target's device so that the attack is concealed [29].

(1.3.2) Forced Re-pairing Attack – A link key is used to establish communication between two Bluetooth devices in the pairing process. This link key is saved in both the devices so that in the ensuing future communications, there is no necessity for verification. The attacker removes the MAC address of any one of the previously paired devices, and subsequently, when the targets try to link the target whose MAC address is not spoofed, it will be forced to re-pair with the attacker device.

(1.3.3) Brute-Force Attack – A brute-force attack skims the MAC address of a Bluetooth device. The attack is utilized on the last 24 bits of MAC address, presuming that the first 24 bits are previously known and fixed [25]. There are roughly 16.8 million probable groupings which will need an average of 8.4 million attempts to attempt. A smart toolkit, which is a free open source software, can be used by the attacker to find it with ease. After determining the target device MAC address, the attacker changes his

MAC address to that of the targets MAC address and snoops the target. In [30], the authors proposed a quicker and effective brute-force procedure, which examines the paging channels linked with the MAC addresses. As a result, it can fix the MAC address of non-discoverable Bluetooth devices.

(1.3.4) Blue-Chop – A Blue-Chop attack creates trouble (no stealing or altering of files) in the established Bluetooth piconet by spoofing the Bluetooth device address of an arbitrary device that is previously operating. This attack is only conceivable if the piconet's master device supports multiple connections [26]. As soon as the attacker spoofs a random slave out of the piconet, it makes way inside the piconet, and contacts the master of the piconet. This leads to misperception of the master's internal state and upsets the piconet, it uninterruptedly sends a connection appeal to all the devices instigating a disturbance and clogs the piconet; which, hinders the steady flow of communication of that piconet. This attack has general validity and is not specific to any device manufacturer.

(1.4) Treacherous Attack – Treacherous attacks are based on launching a trusted relation between the devices and then breaching the trust by taking full control of the target device.

(1.4.1) Backdoor Attack – The backdoor attack gains the target devices by the pairing mechanism. The attacker's device is not visible on the target's list of paired devices and keeps a vigilant watch on the activities of the target device, shown in Figure 7.5. The attacker can collect data from the target device and entry services such as modems, Internet, WAP and GPRS gateways, etc. unaware of the presence of the target [25]. Colleen [31]. The attacker uses the victim's services as if it were an authentic user of it. For this to be successful, the victim device has to be susceptible to a backdoor attack.

(1.4.2) Blue-Bump /Key Bumping – Blue-Bump is a communal/social engineering technique. The attack starts with the attacker sending a text, image, video, or business card to the target device and forcing the receiver to authenticate (Mode-3-Abuse). Upon gaining trust, the attacker coaxes the target to erase the link key that was established during the operation by keeping the connection open. Whereas the target is oblivious of the open connection, the attacker appeals the target to create another link-key. The attacker device remains masked in the paired list of the target device and remains linked with the target without having to authenticate again. To the target the attacker device appears as a completely new device [26]. The attacker is then able to link to the device at any time as long as the key is not deleted again.

(1.5) DoS (Denial of Service) Attacks – DoS attack is a harmless attack and does not rob or modify the target's information. For a brief time, it does not permit the resources of the target device to be available. It either jams the network or generates needless traffic to the network and disturbs the targets. It is dreadful to avert the DoS attack. There are six different types of DoS attacks which are listed next.

(1.5.1) MAC Address Duplication Attack – A MAC address duplication attack is a hacking technique targeting the device address of the target. The attacker replicates itself by means of the stolen MAC Address. The attacker device is positioned in the communication range of the target device. Each and every time any device tries to create a communication with the target, they misguidedly connect to the attacker.

(1.5.2) SCO (Synchronous Connection Oriented link)/eSCO (Enhanced Synchronous Connection Oriented link) Attack – The Synchronous Connection Oriented radio link upholds a set of earmarked timeslots on a prevailing piconet. Being an advanced version, the Enhanced Synchronous Connection Oriented link, is an advanced version of SCO. The SCO/eSCO attack reserves a major chunk of a Bluetooth piconet, due to which, the devices connected in that piconet will not obtain the chosen service in due time.

(1.5.3) Battery Exhaustion Attack or Sleep Deprivation Attack – The battery power of the Bluetooth devices are drained out from the target device [32,33] by attacking the target device's processor and overwhelms the processor making the system unbalanced

(1.5.4) Big NAK (Negative Acknowledgment) Attack – This attack positions the target device in an endless loop of retransmission, due to which the performance of the target device diminishes. The attacker requests data from the target and when the target replies, the attacker states that it has yet to get a response by conveying a negative acknowledgment. Consequently, the target enters into an endless loop of retransmission and keeps on retransmitting and hence it shows that it is busy throughout.

(1.5.5) Guaranteed Service Attack – In a guaranteed service attack, the attacker stresses the attention from the target by demanding the maximum data rate with minimum delay from the target device. Due to this, other devices that are already linked to the target device are disregarded. This attack is preordained to cause trouble in the piconet.

(1.5.6) Blue-Smack Attack – A BlueSmack attack blows out some Bluetooth-enabled devices instantly. This Denial of Service attack is directed using standard tools that ship with the official Linux Bluez utils package. Bluetooth's L2CAP protocol proposes both connection-oriented and connectionless data services. L2CAP requests and obtains data through a L2CAP ping and the magnitude of L2CAP ping of each Bluetooth device is limited. When a L2CAP ping packet is beyond the size of the L2CAP ping size, the system will smash down, and it leads to inoculation of malicious codes [34].

The **l2ping** that ships with the standard distribution of the BlueZ utils permits the user to lay down a packet length that is directed to the respective peer. This is completed by means of the **-s < num >** option. Numerous iPaqs react immediately starting with a size of about 600 bytes.

(1.6) Surveillance – The surveillance attacks watch the target carefully to extract information about the target device. Mostly, the surveillance attacks are not detrimental, but garner information for future attacks.

(1.6.1) Blue-Printing – A Blue-Printing attack is used to find the details of a Bluetooth-enabled device, such as International Mobile Equipment Identity (IMEI) number, manufacturer name, manufacturer details, device model, and firmware version run on the target device [25], unique (Bluetooth device address), manufacturer specific (the first part of the Bluetooth device address), or model-specific (service description records). It does not gain access to steal any information or do any harm to the target device. The attacker gathers the information about a target device by using the Blue-Printing attack to plot an additional attack on that device.

The **Bluetooth Device Address** is exclusive and is made up of 6 bytes (usually penned like MAC addresses MM:MM:MM:XX: XX:XX). This address is the hardware address that is hard-coded in the chipset of the device. The first 3 bytes of this address indicates the manufacturer of the chipset.

(1.6.2) Blue-Stumbling – The Blue-Stumbling method is used to arbitrarily search for Bluetooth devices to pursue and is the first step to initiate an attack. No harm is done to the target. It is frequently done in jam-packed places where a large number of Bluetooth devices are present. The attacker mainly hunts the target and marks the device with more security error that is easy to hack.

(1.6.3) Blue-Tracking – The Blue-Tracking method tracks and follows the target to detect the targets house address or workplace address by tracking the signal of the targets Bluetooth Device. A data set is arrived at by observing and analyzing the target for a few days, so that even the whereabouts of the target can be determined at different period of the day. It does not gain access to steal any information of the target device.

(1.7) Miscellaneous Attack – Assorted attacks comprise burglary of the targeted device data, spying and taking full control of the target device, conducting a spam attack by transferring unsolicited messages, beating the Bluetooth-based car multimedia kit, horse-riding the headset and initiating calls, etc.

(1.7.1) Blue-Snarfing – A Blue-Snarfing attack gains access of target device without permission and retrieves its possessions like contact book, text messages, calendar, emails, document files, pictures, and videos or any contents of the phone memory [25]. It averts an incoming call or text message to the attacker's device without the consent of the target. Blue-Snarfing is illustrated in Figure 7.7 and was identified by Marcel Holtmann in September 2003 [26] who spotted this attack.

(1.7.2) Blue-Snarfing ++ - Blue-Snarfing ++ is an advanced version of Blue-Snarfing and not only robs resources and diverts incoming call or text message but gives full read/write access when connecting to the OBEX Push Profile; it even modifies the stored files in the target device without their consent. It is proficient enough to attain the international mobile equipment identity (IMEI) of the target device. The devices run an OBEX FTP server and can be linked as the OBEX Push service without pairing. Now the attacker can view all files in the filesystem (ls command) and can also erase them (rm command). The filesystem embraces eventual memory extensions like memory sticks or SD cards.

(1.7.3) Blue-Bugging – The Blue-Bugging attacker takes full control of the target device and can do anything according to his or her desires. Blue-Bugging is an attack on the target's privacy and results in resource damage and fiscal injury to the target [25,35,36]. The Blue-Bugging attack creates a serial connection to the phone, permitting access to all the encompassed AT commands. It uses the AT (address translation) commands available in GSM phones, and within approximately 2 seconds, the attacker is able to monitor conversations of nearby phones, and there is no trace of its intrusion.

(1.7.4) Blue-Jacking – Blue-Jacking is a harmless attack and is used for guerrilla marketing to publicize products or services, wherein a text message, image, audio clip, video clip, or electronic business card is sent to the target device. The attacker sends unsolicited messages to target Bluetooth devices and is actually spam and creates an annoyance to the target [25,37–39]. It uses the ——*obex push attack* vulnerability and is reported from many of the Nokia, Sony and Motorola mobile phones.

(1.7.5) Free Calling – The attacker targets the desired Bluetooth device by pairing a headset with a Bluetooth system to make free mobile calls. The attacker overhears not only the targeted persons conversation but also makes them pay for the cost of the call.

(1.7.6) Car Whisperer – In the Car Whisperer attack, the attacker can deceive the targeted car by sending audio to the car stereo system [11] like bogus traffic information and erroneous steering, over-hearing the conversations of the individuals talking inside the car.

(2) MISCELLANEOUS

WAR NIBBLING – Using, laptops or PCs with high gain an-tennas and special software, such as Redfang, the vulnerable Bluetooth phones are tested and attacked, remaining stationary, war nibblers move around mapping as many phones as possible. Some drive and some move from café to café, but the results are the same—they often violate the security of large numbers of consumers.

(3) Worm attack/*BlueBug*||, John Oats (2004); F-Secure Article on Lasco; Ford-Long Wong et al. (2005)] - The self-repeating nature of the worms is used to spread from one Bluetooth device to another Bluetooth device. Upon activation, the worm automatically searches for another Bluetooth devices in range and transmits the.sis file on the target device. Like the Trojan files, the attacker is able to perform all the legal activities with a phone.

BD_ADDR duplication attack: A bug is placed in the range of the target device, which copies the targets BD_ADDR. The Bluetooth Device Address (or BD_ADDR) is an exclusive 48-bit identifier allocated to each Bluetooth device by the manufacturer. When the target device is linked to by any Bluetooth device, either the target device or both devices will reply and logjam each other. Thus, it leads to denial of access from the legitimate device. If the BD_ADDR of the piconet master device is duplicated, then all the information within the piconet goes through the master device and this attack becomes very effective.

L2CAP Guaranteed Service attack: An attacker achieves the maximum bandwidth/highest possible data rate or the smallest/lowest latency performance possible latency from the target device so that all other connections are refused and the throughput is reserved for the attacker. It is also used as a **battery exhaustion attack**. The objective of an attacker is to probe the account, increased challenge, status, thrill, financial gain, damage, and the like. The action of attack can be authenticate, bypass, flood, modify, network, probe, read, scan, spoof, and the like. This attack action/operation results in target actions, increased access, disclosure of information, corruption of information, denial of service, and theft of resources.

Fuzzing - Fuzzing interference encompasses the transfer of distorted or non-standard data to a device's Bluetooth radio and perceiving how the device responds. The targeted device response is slackened or stopped by this attack, and this is due to the vulnerability in the protocol stack [40].

BlueBorne – A BlueBorne attacker exploits apprehensive implementations of Bluetooth on most platforms (Linux devices, Android devices, Amazon and Google home devices) to control or extract data remotely [BlueBorne].

MultiBlue – The MultiBlue dongle is actually a Bluetooth device (4 GB thumb drive), and the MultiBlue application is used to send pairing requests to discoverable nodes. The targeted device presents a code (a pre-shared key) that is used as an authentication key by the

MultiBlue application. The attacker now has access and full node control [41].

Cabir worm – The Cabir worm is a malevolent software that utilizes the Bluetooth technology to hunt for accessible Bluetooth devices and send them to the attacker. The user has to manually admit the worm and mount the malware in order to contaminate the phone. The Mabir worm is basically a variant of the Cabir worm which uses Bluetooth and Multimedia Messaging Service messages (MMS) to duplicate.

Helemoto – The HeloMoto attack is a blend of the BlueSnarf attack and the BlueBug attack, and it gets its name since it was discovered on Motorola phones. This attack exploits the incorrect implementation of a "trusted device" management on certain phones like Motorola devices. Once the attack begins, the attacker disrupts the transfer process and the target lists the attacker's phone and stores it in its device as the "list of trusted devices" as a trusted device. With an admission in that list, the attacker is able to link to the headset profile without verification. The attacker then associates with the target's phone and issues AT commands [42] (as BlueBug).

BlueDump – BlueDumping is the act of instigating a Bluetooth device to "dump" its warehoused link key, thus providing a chance for key-exchange sniffing to occur. In this attack, the attacker spoofs the BDADDR address of one of the devices and attaches it to the other. In the meantime the attacker has no link key; when the target device appeals authentication, the attacker's device will reply with an "HCI_Link_Key_Request_Negative_Reply," which will, in some cases, cause the target device to erase its individual link key and go into pairing mode.

Blooover – Blooover is a proof-of-concept tool that is envisioned to run on J2ME-enabled cell phones that seem to be comparably continuous. Blooover tool is as an audit tool to check if the phones and phones of callers are vulnerable and uses the BlueBug-attack. This is called Blooover (derived from Bluetooth Hoover) because the application runs on handheld devices and draws information.

Blooover II – Blooover II is the successor to the Blooover application and is a new version of the mobile phone auditing tool. The Blooover II supports the BlueBug attack and HeloMoto attack

Table 7.6 Vulnerability and Types of Exploitation

TYPE OF EXPLOITATION	MEANS BY WHICH VULNERABILITY IS EXPLOITED
Autonomous agent	A program, or program fragment, which operates independently from the user.**Examples** - computer viruses or worms.
Data tap	Monitors the electromagnetic radiation originating from a computer or network by means of an external device
Distributed tool	Distributed to multiple hosts, which coordinates to secretly perform an attack on the target host concurrently after some time delay.
Information exchange	A means of gaining information either from other attackers (such as through an electronic bulletin board), or from the people being confronted (commonly called social engineering).
Physical attack	Substantially stealing or damaging a computer, network, its components, or its supporting systems like air conditioning, electric power, etc.
Script or program	By entering commands to a process through the implementation of a file of commands (script) or a program at the process interface.**Examples** - shell script to exploit a software bug, a Trojan horse login program, or a password cracking program.
Toolkit	Software package which contains scripts, programs, or autonomous agents.**Examples** -*rootkit.*
User command	By entering commands to a process through direct user input at the process interface.**Examples** - entering Unix commands through a telnet connection, or commands at an SMTP port.

(which is quite close to the BlueBug attack), the BlueSnarf and the sending of malformed objects via OBEX.

7.8 Bluetooth Vulnerability

A vulnerability is a weakness in a system (computer or network) allowing unauthorized action [43,44]; in order to reach the desired result.

Ivan Victor Krsul [45] shows that a vulnerability in software is a mistake that arises in diverse stages of development or use. This description ends up with three categories of vulnerabilities as follows:

- **Configuration vulnerability** – This vulnerability arises from an error in the configuration of a system, such as partaking system accounts with default passwords, taking "world write" permission for new files, or having vulnerable services enabled [46].

- **Design vulnerability** – This vulnerability is intrinsic in the design or specification of hardware or software whereby even a faultless operation will affect in a vulnerability.
- **Implementation vulnerability** – This vulnerability arises from a fault made in the software or hardware operation of a satisfactory design.

Bluetooth vulnerabilities result in the following:

- The unit key turns into public after its first use
- Encryption keystream repetition
- Paves way for eavesdropping
- PIN management
- Recurrent authentication attempts
- Secure storage of link keys

Vulnerabilities in All Versions of Bluetooth

Cope, P. et al. [47] points out that the following vulnerabilities are prevalent in all versions of Bluetooth:

- Adversaries can view and hypothetically alter link keys if they are stored inappropriately.
- The small key length of the encryption key makes them vulnerable to attackers.
- The encryption keys can be as minor as 1 byte.
- Lack of user authentication.
- Only device authentication is included in the Bluetooth standard
- A device can continue in discoverable/connectable mode for an unlimited period of time.

7.9 Bluetooth Risk Mitigation

Bluetooth attackers use the loopholes/flaws in these devices to steal data, send messages, make phone calls, and connect to the Internet using the target's device. By using application software patches, these types of vulnerabilities are resolved.

The Bluetooth vulnerabilities need to be mitigated in order to upgrade the device firmware. The result is that many Bluetooth devices will remain susceptible long after a mitigating solution becomes available.

Bluetooth uses wireless communication, and the only way to safeguard that Bluetooth communication between the two devices is to pair the devices in a Faraday cage.

Though there is no way to stop all attacks and guarantee security, a number of countermeasures can be used to provide rational security for Bluetooth communications.

A few mitigation techniques are described here:

- Educate Bluetooth users with a suitable level of understanding and awareness and proper security practices.
- Alter the default settings on devices to best standards.
- Bluetooth devices are set to the lowest power level in order to ensure it lies within a secure range.
- Choose sufficiently long and random PIN codes and avoid static and weak PINs that are more resistant to brute-force attacks.
- Link keys should be grounded on combination keys to prevent man-in-the-middle attacks.
- Always set the Bluetooth device in invisible mode, except if it is paired.
- To avert eavesdropping, use link encryption for all data transmissions.
- Ensure that every link is encryption-enabled if multihop communication is used.
- Guarantee that all devices on a network are legitimate by demanding mutual authentication for all accesses.
- To safeguard from being intercepted, encrypt all broadcast transmissions.
- To safeguard from brute-force attacks, use the maximum encryption key size.
- To safeguard from brute-force attacks, set a large minimum key size (preferably 128 bit) for all key negotiation processes.
- Inactivate the Bluetooth devices when not in use to reduce the exposure to threats.
- Only on need, pair the devices and users must be aware of the likelihood of eavesdropping.
- As Security Mode 3 is the highest level of security (as it takes

place at the link level, prior to link establishment) it is highly recommended.

- If a Bluetooth device is lost or stolen, it should be unpaired from any earlier paired devices to avert an attacker from using the missing device to access any of the owner's other Bluetooth devices.
- Always avoid and do not accept transmissions of any kind (messages, files, and images) from unknown or suspicious devices and accept content only from trusted devices.

7.10 Countermeasures

The technology evolution and the evolution of attacks are going at the same speed. The efforts taken to develop countermeasures against all the weaknesses and the security holes of Bluetooth are still in their infancy. The weakest part of the Bluetooth technology comprises the pairing process in which it rests on the trusted relationships with other devices.

To address the specific threats and vulnerabilities to Bluetooth network, countermeasures should be applied.

- Educate Bluetooth-enabled device users with an appropriate level of knowledge, understanding, and awareness of proper security practices. For example, organizations should create an awareness-based education to its staff to improve their understanding and knowledge of Bluetooth.
- Design and document the security policies that should be used by the organizations adopting Bluetooth technology and users of the Bluetooth-enabled devices should understand their responsibilities.

Security checklist with guiding principle and suggestions for forming and maintaining secure Bluetooth piconets:

- Ensure that an organizational wireless security policy is developed to addresses the Bluetooth technology.
- Ensure that users of the Bluetooth technology are cognizant of their security-related responsibilities concerning Bluetooth use.

- Perform a thorough security assessments at regular intervals to fully realize the organization's Bluetooth security posture.
- Confirm that wireless devices and networks linking Bluetooth technology are completely understood from an architecture viewpoint and documented consequently.
- Provide the users with a checklist of precautionary measures to be adhered with for better protection of handheld Bluetooth devices from theft.
- Modify the default settings of the Bluetooth device to mirror the organization's security policy.
- Bluetooth devices are set to the lowest power level in order to ensure they lie within a secure perimeter of the organization.
- Install and update an antivirus software on Bluetooth-enabled hosts that are regularly beleaguered by malware.
- Fully test and install Bluetooth software patches and upgrades frequently.

The **countermeasures** are classified into five generic categories as follows:

- **Access Control & Authentication:** Employ access control and authentication methods to prevent attacks aiming at the confidentiality, integrity, and availability. **Access controls** that can be used are user access controls (role-based access control, location-based access control, supervisory access control, reactive access control), access control of overprivileged applications, default-off access control, access control with delegation, data flow control. **Authentications** like continuous authentication mechanism work well.
- **Intrusion Detection and Mitigation:** Use the right intrusion detection systems (IDSs) to detect malicious behavior, and possibly mitigate the attacks targeting confidentiality, integrity, and availability. The use of intrusion detection and mitigation can be based on detecting side-channel attacks, detecting the execution of malicious processes, detecting routing attacks, detecting event spoofing attacks, detecting voice-command injection attacks, detecting attacks via encrypted traffic analysis, and detecting hidden inter-application interactions.

- **Security Protocols and Frameworks:** Utilize the verified and validated appropriate proposed security protocols and frameworks in order to address the unique challenges of securing the environments.
- **Software Reliability:** The software reliability is ensured through code verification, automatic updates, software testing through fuzzing and rapid patching, reliable patching, and update mechanisms.
- **Identification and Management:** Identify and troubleshoot mismanaged or misconfigured Bluetooth and paired devices by using proper identification and management techniques like identification through traffic analysis, secure logging, management of compromised devices, and traffic shaping to prevent unauthorized identification.

7.11 Conclusion

Bluetooth's acceptance has grown leaps and bounds, as it is an easy convenient solution to establish a wireless link and transfers files/videos, voice, and data between mobile devices in a short range. Bluetooth offers a viable solution to numerous devices that might not have wireless connectivity without it, like better communication channels, clear user interface, and interaction, using a policy. The 15-year-old technology has become the go-to, convenient solution for connecting devices, including phones, cameras, televisions, speakers, headphones, smartwatches, and medical devices, as well as personal assistants.

The Bluetooth is a secure standard (per se), and the Bluetooth technology uses inbuilt enhanced security techniques for trustworthiness of data transfer. Only a limited literature explains the Bluetooth attacks, and the prevailing surveys on Bluetooth security sketch only a limited attack deprived of classification, and people are not much mindful of them.

The objective of this chapter is to provide a comprehensive survey of existing attacks, threats, and vulnerabilities in Bluetooth technology and suggest probable solutions. In this chapter, the Bluetooth security, security services and features are deliberated. The security vulnerabilities in various versions of Bluetooth, which are largely due to the process of pairing, that are affecting Bluetooth technology, as well as Bluetooth-connected devices, have been analyzed. The numerous Bluetooth threats, prevalent in the various versions of Bluetooth, especially which are largely due to the process of pairing have been discussed.

An examination of the Bluetooth risk mitigation techniques that can be used to shield the Bluetooth commercial products or devices and information from attackers was discussed, as well as recommendations on how to secure Bluetooth communications. Realizing the endorsed security measures will help to alleviate any Bluetooth-related risks. The Bluetooth device manufacturers are proactively trying to keep the technology secure, but the cycle is incomplete without the contribution of the end users, who must be aware of these security threats and take a minimum level of precaution. As there is no one trusted, central party to necessary action, the Bluetooth users should be responsible for securing their Bluetooth communications, besides following the countermeasures.

There are still unsolved BT challenges from the security point of view. The up-to-date current countermeasures still lack deficiencies, which, when eradicated, will definitely offer the desired degree of effectiveness.

7.12 Future Work

To efficiently get rid of the problem, research now has to shift emphasis to a more essential update of the existing Bluetooth structure. The future direction for research will be to focus on a new theory targeting to stop MITM attacks at the grass root level.

The ***process and the structure of the pairing*** is another area of research. From a theoretical point of view, only the necessary information to research a pairing structure for Bluetooth that is devoid of the traditional Secure Simple Pairing method, but also a structure that pre-serves/improves the current level of practicality and user friendliness in the technology all the while closing any possible security gaps to finally allow users to enjoy the full potential of Bluetooth without having to make any compromises.

Next suggestion would be to change the communications from a device-based source (as it is exposed to external infiltrations) to a virtual channel-based exchange. Another promising direction is to propose, new countermeasures to enhance "just work" model which is the gap that the attacker exploits to start the attack. The future direction for research will be to improve in such a way that all the emails linked to that keyword should be recognized and displayed. Another promising direction is to reduce the research gap by developing better protocols so that Bluetooth's vulnerability is handled. The next promising direction of research will be to potentially focus on power attacks on BLE, as it is targeted for low-energy applications.

References

1. BlueBorne. Available online: https://armis.com/blueborne/ (accessed on 18 July 2019).
2. Clover, Juli. 2020. https://itechblog.co/bluetooth-sig-announces-le-audio-with-audio-sharing-lower-data-consumption-hearing-aid-support-and-more/
3. Estimote, Inc., "Indoor Location with Bluetooth and Mesh," "https://estimote.com/", [Online]; accessed 29-Nov-2018.
4. F. Zafari and I. Papapanagiotou, "Enhancing iBeacon Based Micro-Location with Particle Filtering," in 2015 IEEE Global Communications Conference (GLOBECOM), 12 , pp. 1–7, 2015.
5. F-Secure Article on Lasco. A Worm, available at: http://www.f-secure.com/v-descs/lasco
6. D. K. Oka, T. Furue, L. Langenhop, and T. Nishimura, "Survey of Vehicle IoT Bluetooth Devices," in 2014 IEEE 7th International Conference on Service-Oriented Computing and Applications (SOCA), vol. 00, Nov. 2014, pp. 260–264. [Online]. Available: oi.ieeecomputersociety.org/10.1109/SOCA.2014.20
7. R. Bouhenguel, I. Mahgoub, and M. Ilyas, "Bluetooth Security in Wearable Computing Applications," in *2008 International Symposium on High Capacity Optical Networks and Enabling Technologies*, Nov 2008, pp. 182–186.
8. Monson, Heidi - "Bluetooth Technology and Implications" available at: http://www.sysopt.com/features/network/article.php/3532506 (1999-12-14).
9. Mohammed Mana, Mohammed Feham, and Boucif Amar Bensaber, "A light weight protocol to Provide location privacy in wireless body area networks", *International Journal of Network Security and its Applications (IJNSA)*, vol. 3, no. 2, 2011 International Journal of Distributed and Parallel Systems (IJDPS) Vol. 3, No. 1, January 2012.
10. Nateq Be-Nazir Ibn, M. and Tarique, M. Bluetooth security threats and solutions: A survey. *International Journal of Distributed Parallel Systems*, vol. 3, p. 127, 2012.
11. T. Panse and P. Panse, "A survey on security threats and vulnerability attacks on bluetooth communication," *International Journal of Computer Science and Information Technologies*, vol. 4, no. 5, pp. 741–746, 2013.
12. Hassan, S.S., Bibon, S.D., Hossain, M.S. and Atiquzzzaman, M. "Security Threats in Bluetooth Technology." *Computers & Security*, vol. 74, pp. 308–322, 2017.
13. Darroudi, S.M. and Gomez, C. "Bluetooth low energy mesh networks: A survey." *Sensors*, vol. 17, pp. 1467, 2017.
14. Zhiqiang Lin, (2019) https://www.sciencedaily.com/releases/2019/11/191114124048.htm
15. Zou, Y., Wang, X. and Hanzo, L. A survey on wireless security: Technical challenges, recent advances and future trends. arXiv 2015, arxiv:1505.07919.

16. K. Scarfone and J. Padgette. "Guide to Bluetooth security," Tech. Rep., 2008.
17. R. Brooks, S. Sander, J. Deng, and J. Taiber. "Automobile security concerns," *IEEE Vehicular Technology Magazine*, vol. 4, no. 2, pp. 52–64, 2009.
18. J. D. Howard and T. A. Longstaff, "A common language for computer security incidents," Sandia National Laboratories, Tech. Rep. SAND98-8667, 1998.
19. John Oates, ——Virus attacks mobiles via Bluetooth‖, available at: http://www.theregister.co.uk/ 2004/06/15/symbian_virus8/
20. Jun-Zhao Sun, Douglas Howie, Antti Koivisto and Jaakko Sauvola. Media Team, Machine Vision and Media Processing unit, InfoTech Oulu, University of Oulu, Finland, ——Design Implementation and Evaluation of Bluetooth security.
21. V. Verendel, D. K. Nilsson, U. E. Larson, and E. Jonsson. "An approach to using honeypots in in-vehicle networks," in 68th Vehicular Technology Conf. Calgary, Canada: IEEE, 2008, pp. 1–5.
22. Wuling Ren, Zhiqian Miao, College of Computer and Information Engineering, Zhejiang Gongshang University, ——A Hybrid Encryption Algorithm Based on DES and RSA" in Bluetooth Communication Second International Conference on Modeling, Simulation and Visualization Methods, 2010.
23. Y. Shaked and A. Wool, "Cracking the Bluetooth PIN," in 3rd international conference on Mobile systems, applications, and services. New York, USA: ACM, 2005, pp. 39–50.
24. D. K. Nilsson, P. A. Porras, and E. Jonsson, "How to secure Bluetooth-based pico networks," in International Conference on Computer Safety, Reliability, and Security. Nurmberg, Germany: Springer, , pp. 209–223, 2007.
25. N. B.-N. I. Minar and M. Tarique, "Bluetooth security threats and solutions: a survey," *International Journal of Distributed and Parallel Systems*, vol. 3, no. 1, 2012.
26. M. Herfurt and C. Mulliner, "Bluetooth security vulnerabilities and bluetooth projects," Web page, 2005. [Online]. Available: http://trifinite.org/trifinite_stuff.html
27. P. M. Raphael and C.-W. Phan, "Analyzing the secure simple pairing in bluetooth v4.0," *Wireless Personal Communications*, vol. 64, no. 4, pp. 719–737, 2012.
28. S. Sandhya and K. A. S. Devi, "Contention for man-in-the-middle attacks in Bluetooth networks," in International Conference on Computational Intelligence and Communication Networks. Mathura, Uttar Pradesh, India: IEEE, Nov 3–5, pp. 700–703, 2012.
29. Computer Security PGP, "MAC address spoofing for bluetooth," Blog, Feb 2016. [Online]. Available: http://computersecuritypgp.blogspot.com/2016/02/mac-address-spoofing-for-bluetooth.html

30. D. Cross, J. Hoeckle, M. Lavine, J. Rubin, and K. Snow, "Detecting non-discoverable bluetooth devices," *International Federation for Information Processing*, vol. 253, pp. 281–293, 2008.

31. R. Colleen, "Bluetooth security," *Technical Report, East Carolina University*, pp. 6–9, 2006.

32. S. N. Premnath and S. K. Kasera, "Battery-draining-denial-of-service attack on Bluetooth devices," Technical poster, 2008.

33. S. Pasanen, "New efficient rf fingerprint-based security solution for bluetooth secure simple pairing," *Security*, pp. 1–8, 2010.

34. D. Strobel, "IMSI catcher," *Technical report, Ruhr-Universit Bochum*, 2007.

35. G. Legg, "The bluejacking, bluesnarfing, bluebugging blues: Bluetooth faces perception of vulnerability," Web page, 2005. [Online]. Available: http://www.eetimes.com/document.asp

36. Garbelini, M. E., Chattopadhyay, S., & Wang, C. "LL Encryption procedure". *Channels*, vol. 37, no. 38, p. 39.

37. M. Tan and K. A. Masagca, "An investigation of bluetooth security threats," in International Conference on Information Science and Applications. Jeju Island, Republic of Korea: IEEE, 26–29 April, 2011.

38. M. Wolf, A. Weimerskirch, and C. Paar, "Security in automotive bus systems," in 2nd Embedded Security in Cars Workshop (ESCAR 2004), Bochum, Germany, 2004, pp. 11–12.

39. Markus Jakobsson and Susanne Vitzel, Lucent Technologies – Bell Bell Labs, Information Science Research Center, Murray Hill, USA, Security Weakness in Bluetooth‖.

40. Tsira, V. and Nandi, G. "Bluetooth Technology: Security Issues and its Prevention." International Journal of Computer Applications in Technology, vol. 5, pp. 1833–1837, 2014.

41. Lonzetta, A., Cope, P., Campbell, J. and Mohd, B. "Security Vulnerabilities in Bluetooth Technology as used in IoT." Journal of Sensor and Actuator Networks, vol. 7, p. 28, 2018.

42. Browing, D. and Kessler, G. Bluetooth Hacking: A Case Study. Available online: https://www.garykessler.net/library/bluetooth_hacking_browning_kessler.pdf (accessed on 7 September 2019).

43. Edward G. Amoroso, Fundamentals of Computer Security Technology, Prentice-Hall PTR, Upper Saddle River, NJ, 1994.

44. National Research Council, Computers at Risk: Safe Computing in the Information Age, National Academy Press, Washington, DC, 1991.

45. Ivan Victor Krsul, Software Vulnerability Analysis, Ph.D. Dissertation, Computer Sciences Department, Purdue University, Lafayette, IN, 1998.

46. Derek Atkins, Paul Buis, Chris Hare, Robert Kelley, Carey Nachenberg, Anthony B. Nelson, Paul Phillips, Tim Ritchey, and William Steen. "Internet Security Professional Reference", New Riders Publishing, IN, 1996.

47. Cope, P.; Campbell, J.; Hayajneh, T. An Investigation of Bluetooth Security Vulnerabilities. In Proceedings of the 7th IEEE Annual Computing and Communication Workshop and Conference (IEEE CCWC 2017), Las Vegas, NV, USA, 2017.

INDEX

Printed in the United States
By Bookmasters